Making *true* Love

A Guide to
Lasting Relationships

By Thomas and Donna Finn

Illustrated by Chris Ware

Pauline
BOOKS & MEDIA
Boston

Nihil Obstat:
    Rev. Msgr. Richard G. Cunningham, J.C.D.
Imprimatur:
    ✠ Bernard Cardinal Law
    Archbishop of Boston
    July 16, 2001

Library of Congress Cataloging-in-Publication Data

Finn, Thomas.
    Making true love : a guide to lasting relationships / Thomas and
Donna Finn.
        p.   cm.
    ISBN 0-8198-4811-5
    1.   Sex — Religious aspects — Catholic Church.   2.   Love —
Religious aspects — Catholic Church.   3.   Catholic Church —
Doctrines.   I. Finn, Donna.   II. Title.
    BX1795.S48 F57 2001

    241'.66 — dc21

                                                        2001002598

Printed and published in the U.S.A. by Pauline Books & Media, 50 Saint
Pauls Avenue, Boston, MA 02130–3491.

Pauline Books & Media is the publishing house of the Daughters of
St. Paul, an international congregation of women religious serving the
Church with the communications media.

1 2 3 4 5 6 7 8 9   05 04 03 02 01

Dedication

To John and Sue Brennan, whose love for one another has been a living testimony to the reality of sacramental love and the presence of God's love in our world. We have been honored to share in your journey.

Contents

Preface   1

ORIENTATION

Chapter 1:   The Journey of Love   5

Chapter 2:   What Is True Love?

The Looks of Love   8
True Love   10
Love: Commitment to Action   11
Sexuality   13
Two Different Trails   15
Which Path to Take?   17

PREPARATIONS FOR THE JOURNEY

Chapter 3:   Who Am I and Where Have I Been?

Understanding Ourselves   22
Understanding Our Hopes for Love   24
Understanding the Roots of Our Expectations   25
Family Relationships   25
We Learn What We See   27
Social Relationships   29
Media   32
Church   33

Chapter 4: Misconceptions of Love

Love Is Only a Feeling   36
Love Is Sex   38
Love Is Security   38
Messing with Nature   39

Chapter 5: The Dynamic Progression of Love

The Sexual Urge   42
Attraction   43
Desire   45
Oh, What a Feeling!   46
Goodwill and Friendship   48
Friendship   48
Betrothed Love   49
Is Surrender a Good Thing?   50
The Actions of True Love   51
A Breather   55

EXPERIENCING THE JOURNEY

Chapter 6: Experiences and Reference Points

Our Experience of Love   59
Reference Points   61
An Examination of Relationship Conscience   61

Chapter 7: Relationship Beginnings and Boundaries

Our Attraction Reactions   65
The Boundaries of Desire   69
Time Together   69
But You Make Me Feel So Good!   70

Chapter 8: Am I in Love?

Infatuation   72

Words of Love   73
Infatuation versus Love   75
Falling in Love   76

**Chapter 9: Compatibility, Communication
              and Closeness**

A Relationship Compass   77
Compatibility   78
Into Intimacy   80
Communication   81
Physical Closeness   83
Friendship or Sex?   84

Chapter 10: Chastity

A New Perspective   87
One Word Is Worth a Thousand Pictures   89
Virtual Effort   90
Loving Service   90
The Road to Oneness   91
Self-Mastery   92
Freedom   92
Chastity Or?   94

Chapter 11: Sex Effects

Choice Influences   95
External Influences   95
Internal Influences   97
Nonmarital Sex and Problems
    on a Personal Level   98
Problems on a Social Level   101
Cohabitation   102
The Role of Pornography   103
Sex and Your Spirit   104

Chapter 12: Sex and Spirituality

Sign Language 105
God Signs 106
Sex as Testimony 108
Homosexuality 110
Problems on a Spiritual Level 112
Lust versus Love 112
False Witness 114
"Partners" 115
Just Call Me "Bond" 116
Moving Toward Chastity 117

Chapter 13: Choosing Chastity

A Changing Perspective 118
Chastity in Action 119
What If I've Already Had Sex? 121
A Last Word on Chastity 123
Where Are We, Anyway? 124

Chapter 14: Friendship and Betrothed Love

From "I" to "We" 125
Seeds or Weeds? 126
Lovers' Leap: Betrothed Love 128

Chapter 15: When Relationships Don't Work Out

Feeling a Grind 131
Conflict 132
Intuition 133
Can We Work It Out? 134
Physical Violence and Emotional Abuse 136
Dead Ends 137
Second Chances 139
Self-Defeating Reactions 140

Panic and Aloneness   141
Depression   141
Rebounds   142
Offensive and Defensive Rebounds   142
Controlling the Rebounds   143
Can We Still Be Friends?   144

Chapter 16: Sexual Assault
Traumatic Experiences   145
Safety in Numbers   146
Bottoms Up, Lids On   148

THE JOURNEY HOME

Chapter 17: The Big Picture of Love's Journey
A Review   154
True and Lasting Love   155
The Importance of Guides   156
Respecting Respect   157

Chapter 18: The Final Destination
Testimony to True Love   159
The Depths of True Love   163
No Greater Love   165
Destination: God   166
Truth, Faith and the Commandment to Love   166

Notes   169

Appendix—Further Reading for the Journey   173

Acknowledgments

To all who have offered help and ideas for *Making True Love*, we offer our sincere thanks. We would like to particularly thank Sr. Mary Mark, FSP, and the Daughters of St. Paul for your invitation to produce this work, your ideas for content and your willingness to redefine the concept of a deadline.

Our thanks also to Tom and Jeanne Ouimet, for showing us through your life and words how to trust God, hear his call and have the courage to follow it.

To our parents for setting the foundation of faith upon which our marriage, family life and work has been built, and to the couples with whom we have shared circles of prayer and fellowship. You have been sources of inspiration while providing many of the trail markers on our personal journey of love.

Preface

Journey. Perhaps this is the best word to describe the experience of love. When we think about other kinds of journeys — whether it be a vacation, a business trip, a new school year, a new job, and so on — we understand that we will be walking a trail from one place to another, and in doing so, will encounter both challenge and transformation. The same holds true for the journey of love — the greatest human adventure of all.

Realistically, the journey of love is not an easy one. It can hold as much sadness, fear, hurt, rejection, loneliness and pain as it does joy, laughter, fulfillment, intimacy and peace. Through all the ups and downs on the path of love, we usually have one destination in mind: a lasting, truly loving relationship with someone with whom we can grow and live out our dreams over a lifetime. Whether you are single, engaged or married, *Making True Love* is intended to be one resource — a trail guide of sorts — in your personal journey toward a loving, lasting relationship. We have tried to capture in brief, concrete terms a dimension of our lives that deserves greater discussion. We hope this book will serve as a springboard for your continued search for a fuller, more meaningful understanding of how to follow God's call to love within the context of human sexuality and male-female love relationships.

Just as nature's rhythm of sunrise to sunset brings with it new discoveries and adventures, the rhythm of love allows us to discover ourselves, our lives and our God in ways that we would never imagine possible. If you are (or would like to be) the type of person who can see in a sunrise or sunset not the beginning or end of a day, but an invitation to seek a deeper knowledge of yourself, of your relationships with others and of your relationship with God, then you are truly a seeker of love and we are honored to share this part of your journey with you. *Bon voyage!*

ORIENTATION

Chapter 1
The Journey of Love

What picture comes to mind when you think of a journey? Maybe it is one of long, winding trails through mountain passes, voyages on the sea, or a minivan filled with camping gear and a full bike rack. Whatever your image might be, the picture of a journey is always framed by a period of time in which we begin in one place, end up in another, and in between experience a fair amount of challenge and growth.

The social culture in which we live has, unfortunately, made it harder to appreciate the fulfillment gained from a journey over time. If we want something, we should be able to have it — *now*. That new car, a big screen TV...get it now, no payments until next year. The stew that filled a home with an aroma of mouth-watering anticipation for hours is now a microwave meal ready in four minutes.

Ultimately, the greatest casualty of the "If you want it, get it now" philosophy has been the distortion of the map that guides the "Journey of Love."

Love in the world's view is primarily a "thing" we are supposed to have in our lives and need in order to be happy — *now*. Love is viewed too simply as a feeling to be

experienced between two people — a feeling benchmarked by experiences of attraction, desire and sexual pleasure occurring within days (maybe weeks) after the start of a relationship. Love lasts only until that feeling is gone, most often when the trail becomes steep and difficult. Love's journey has sadly become a quick trip to temporary happiness and is far from the path of its original design: a lifetime of action, supported and enriched by human emotion, yet benchmarked by self-giving, mutual respect, sacrifice and unconditional commitment that takes two people from fields of romance through valleys of struggle to peaks of true joy.

The fractured picture of love's journey is not surprising given the way our society has drawn it for us since we were children. Surfing through television channels, movie theaters, magazine stands and the like, we see a familiar image of "The Love Express": relationships begun today, "in love" tomorrow, in bed the day after, in court the next year. More subtly, our view of love's journey has also been influenced by the belief that our emotional and sexual "needs" deserve to be met. Phrases such as, "You're not meeting my needs," have become common trail markers leading toward anger, disappointment, infidelity and selfishness. As a result, we become the center of our own attention and the object of our own affections. We end up confused, hurt, alone and unsatisfied, wondering what happened to that "true love" we thought we had.

Luckily, true love can be a reality. It is our humble goal to offer you a broader picture of love, not one designed on our own drawing board of life, but one that sketches God's picture of love as he has drawn it with you as his special subject. Perhaps you are in a love relationship now or have recently ended one, or maybe you have never experienced a love relationship. Whatever your life's story has been to date, we encourage you to explore your own personal journey of love and ask yourself three basic questions:

1. *Where have I been?* What has my experience of love's journey taught me to believe about love?

2. *Where am I now?* How am I acting on these beliefs and expectations in my relationships? What do I need to understand and learn more fully to keep moving toward truly loving relationships?

3. *Where do I want to go?* How do I want my love relationships to be in the future?

Before we can answer these questions fully, however, we need a frame of reference to understand the nature of our journey and give us an initial glimpse of our destination.

Chapter 2
What Is True Love?

We feel somewhat presumptuous attempting to describe true love, given the moral relativity of our world. Today's mainstream generally views the concept of "truth" as a value-laden, freedom-restricting, unrealistic demand. Basically the postmodern world rejects that objective truth exists, preferring to let "truth" be totally subjective — with each individual defining his or her own or even denying its existence. It would be typical if your education and experience of life and love have left you wondering about truth in ways similar to Pilate in the praetorium during the trial of Jesus. Jesus tells Pilate:

"For this I was born and for this I came into the world — to bear witness to the truth. Everyone who is of the truth hears my voice" (Jn 18:37).

Pilate responds: "Truth! What does that mean?" We would trust that you are open to exploring a similar question: "True love! What does that mean?"

The Looks of Love

Thousands of definitions and descriptions of love have been painted over the centuries. They can be found everywhere — from the writings of the greatest poets and authors to the bathroom walls of schools and subways. For our discussion, however, we'll distinguish among four different dimensions of love.

Family Love: Here, the word *love* refers to the natural bond among relatives within a family such as parent-child, cousin-cousin, brother-sister and so on. This type of love holds a warmth and commitment introduced through blood or adoption and developed over the course of a shared history.

Friendship Love: This dimension captures the closeness and respect seen among good friends spanning a spectrum of closeness from better acquaintances to best friendships. There is a tenderness and concern here, but it is not romantic in nature.

Romantic Love: This dimension describes the passionate, sometimes possessive dimension of love that early Greek culture referred to as *eros*, or erotic love. This love is recognized in the power of attraction and desire for another that seeks union with that person, often through sexual expression.

Agape Love: This is the unconditional love a person has for another in which one devotes oneself to the other's fulfillment and seeks the best for that person. In its purest form, it is God's love for each of us: unconditional, permanent and complete.

The lines among these dimensions of love are sometimes blurred and difficult to recognize. For our purposes, when we speak of love we will be focusing mostly on the latter two dimensions, romantic love and agape love, in the context of male-female love relationships. So, if you think, "Hey, wouldn't that also apply in my relationships with my family, my parishioners, my friends and so on?" you would be right. Our intent, however, is to focus on the love relationships between men and women from initial attraction through dating and courtship to marriage.

True Love

We know that we are created in God's image and likeness (Gen 1:26). Since God is Truth (Jn 14:6) and God is Love (1 Jn 4:8), we have the inborn capacity to reflect the truth and love of God. True love, then, is loving the way that God loves all of us — completely, unconditionally and permanently. When we love the way that God loves, we give ourselves permanently to someone in a way that completely and unconditionally honors and respects that person's worth, value and dignity as a human person. That means that our love for a person is to always honor and respect his or her body, mind and spirit in a way that seeks and affirms what is good for that person. In a general sense, seeking that "good" means desiring that person's growth in the ability to reach her or his God-given potential as a human person. It means helping that person love others (including you), in ways that more and more resemble God's complete, unconditional and permanent love.[1]

The respect found in true love honors the other's freedom, perfects that person's life and enlarges the existence of that person.[2] This often requires some degree of sacrifice, but because there is a mutual or shared relationship, your own existence is enriched and enlarged in return. A hallmark of true love is the absence of selfish or ulterior motives on your part (or the other's) that would cause you to use another person for your own physical, psychological or social needs and gain. Using another person for either sexual pleasure, an emotional lift or any other ego boost may or may not be conscious, but it leads to a deterioration of the human spirit and blocks our ability to love in ways true to God's design.

True love transcends personal gain. It is selfless, self-sacrificing, honorable and holistic.[3] True lovers see each other as whole persons, journeying together throughout a lifetime toward deeper union with each other and with God. You won't find the words *fast and easy* anywhere along this journey. This is not the "fast lane" to love.

Love: Commitment to Action

Sometimes it helps to understand some of the dimensions of true love if we consider the way we talk about "truly loving" in a context other than human relationships. For example, take people who "truly love" golf. They spend a lot of time learning the golf swing, the strategy of the game and the rules. They study equipment, read golf magazines and watch golf on TV. They spend a great deal of time practicing sand shots, chips, putts, short irons, long irons and drives, and play often whether they shoot a 66 or a 106. They do this year in and year out, even to the extent that they sacrifice other things in doing their utmost to be the best golfers they can be. In other words, they give themselves to the game because they "truly love" it.

How about people who truly love to garden? They spend a lot of time selecting the right site for their vegetables and flowers and researching the best plants to plant and when to plant them. They consult with other gardeners, read gardening journals and chat in gardening chat rooms. They put great effort into tending their gardens by weeding, spraying, pruning, fertilizing and the like, making whatever sacrifices are necessary. They want their gardens to yield good fruits for their labor and, therefore, invest the time and effort required to make that happen, knowing that sometimes the yield may be sparse. In the end they feel a sense of pride and satisfaction, because they truly love the process of gardening.

Truly loving golf and gardening translates into action. That action involves giving oneself to his or her interest over a long time and being willing to go the distance to get results. It requires patience, acts of self-giving, commitment and self-sacrifice where one would not reasonably expect a positive outcome without such investments.

Okay, so you're not a golfer or gardener, but you are very likely pursuing, have pursued or will someday pursue a vocation. No one actually expects that a meaningful career, ministry, marriage or parenthood, for example, would develop via a magical "poof." We assume, rather, that these will take time, effort, experience and education in order to fulfill our vocations' potential.

If we (your authors) look at our own careers as a psychologist and a physical therapist, we each truly love our chosen work, but each is now nearly twenty-five years in the making. Starting with college, followed by volunteer and practicum work, graduate school, dissertations and theses, internships, first jobs, long hours, new jobs, promotions, continuing education, cutting back to raise children, successes, failures, joys, disillusionments and so on, the journey has been long yet, hopefully, is only in its early stages. Giving of ourselves in our work, commitment and self-sacrifice over a long time...we knew these would be required from the beginning and that the rewards were far up the trail. We didn't expect instant success and we were not even sure what that success would look like once we achieved it.

So whether it's breaking 80 on the golf course, reaping a full harvest from the garden or attaining success in a career, none are accomplished by a fast and easy trip, nor can they be realized without giving oneself to the whole package. There are no instant winners in the lottery of life!

Obviously, on the journey of human love, we are not dealing with golf balls, tomatoes or job descriptions. We are individuals in all of our complexity, and yet many of us assume that lasting, truly loving relationships are supposed to just "happen"! They don't. If you are to truly love and be truly loved, you will need to make the choice to give yourself fully, unconditionally, permanently and unselfishly to another and accept the same in return. True love, at this point in our discussion, is best understood as a faithful love — a committed decision to live for another over a lifetime together.

Sexuality

Any discussion of true love has to include a discussion of sexuality, probably one of the most misunderstood concepts of our time. Too often, when we hear the word *sexuality*, the "uality" becomes invisible and shortened to "sex," that is, genital sex. "Expressing my sexuality" becomes the banner phrase for "having sex," "making love," "sleeping together" or any other route to sexual pleasure.

Sexuality is much more than just attraction, arousal and orgasm. Sexuality is who we are as the male or female person God has created us to be. Think of your sexuality as your identity — the physical, intellectual, emotional, social and spiritual *you* that has never been, and never will be, repeated. Your identity — your sexuality — is a gift that God has given to you with the intent that you honor and express it appropriately on your journey of love.

Expressing your sexuality means being who you are in authentic, honest and mutually respectful relationships with others. Your sexuality is healthy and reflective of God's image when, through your own free will, you choose to love unselfishly for the good of another and reserve the intimate physical dimension of your sexuality for the time when it can truly express the complete, permanent and unconditional giving of yourself to another, that is, in marriage. The holistic quality of true love is present when a man and a woman give themselves spiritually, psychologically, socially, emotionally and physically to one another in a free and mutual decision to help each other grow to their full potentials as persons loving in a God-like way, while reserving complete self-giving on the physical level (i.e., sexual intercourse) until after the wedding.

Understandably, many people follow this discussion with an open mind until they get to that last line! What many people have said that makes sense along the way changes with the words *until marriage*. Reactions include, "C'mon. Are you serious? These are modern times." Yes, we are serious and we'll address all of the reasons why in a later chapter, so we do hope you will stay open to the discussion and read along.

Two Different Trails

To help make this more concrete, let's follow the early journeys of two fictional couples who met at the local health club. Both couples experienced strong feelings of attraction for one another, complete with those usual butterflies, heart flutters and eye-to-eye across-the-room lock-ons, but they took very different trails in response.

Couple #1: He asked her out to dinner several days after they met, and following dessert, they went back to her apartment for coffee. Sitting close together on the couch he kissed her and after a while the light stuff led to French kissing. He left her place about 3:00 A.M.

The next day, she rushed home after work to see if he had left a message on her answering machine, which he had, inviting her to a movie. They went and afterward came back to his place to talk, which they did, followed by kissing and light petting. The next weeks went along with the couple seeing each other at least four to five times a week and, by the end of the fourth week, they were sleeping together (going all the way), and often staying overnight at each other's apartments. They felt marvelously in love, were passionate with each other and felt like soul mates. She knew this was the man she'd always looked for — kind, sensitive, willing to listen to her feelings and past pains of life and able to make her feel special.

After several months, the softball season began. He had games after work almost every other day and on weekends (he played on three teams), and loved to have her come and watch. Following the game and a few beers, they'd return to one of their apartments for a late dinner. She usually cooked or they ordered pizza. They would then go to bed, having sex about four or five times a week.

Two months into the season, she realized they weren't talking as much as they had in the past and began to feel resentful of his softball. She told him, but he angrily told her not to try to control him. She became more angry and hurt and went to fewer games. He began to go out with his teammates more often, coming home late and somewhat buzzed. At least, according to them, sex was good and it made them feel connected and wanted. They began to talk about her moving in with him when her lease expired in three months.

The following week, a friend of hers told her that she had seen him at a bar after a game with another woman. When he came over that night, she confronted him and they had a heated argument that ended with him storming out of the apartment swearing at her for being so possessive and mistrusting. Three weeks later the relationship ended.

Couple #2: For the first couple weeks after they met, they would talk for a time in the health club lobby, and he eventually asked her to coffee after a workout. She agreed and, after coffee, they exchanged phone numbers. He asked her to a movie the next weekend followed by coffee, and they talked about the possibility of seeing each other more often. They agreed to pursue the friendship and talked about things they enjoyed doing, discovering they both enjoyed the outdoors. They saw each other frequently at the gym and began to date once or twice a week, hiking, going to the beach and the like. Dates would end with dinner at local restaurants and after several months, she would invite him home for coffee. They would talk about anything and everything and he would leave around 1:00 A.M. following progressively longer kisses. As their feelings for each other grew, they both were aware of the sexual desire they felt for each other, and they discussed it one night. They concluded with an agreement that they would honor the respect they felt for each other and not go any farther physically as they valued their relationship too much to risk hurting it.

Which Path to Take?

Whether or not you think either scenario is realistic, both happen and reflect totally different ways of handling the early months of a relationship. Couple #1 follows the "fast lane," the "get it now" road. This trail is marked with infatuation, neediness, self-centeredness, selfishness, immediate gratification, pleasure seeking, utility (using a person as an object), emotional volatility, dishonesty and convenience. Couple #2 follows the "middle lane," the "take-it-slow-to-lasting-relationships" road. This lane is marked with patience, respect, self-control, self-confidence, other-centeredness, open communication, emotional balance, acceptance, knowledge and honesty. Following different trails will ultimately lead to very, very different destinations if the same types of trail markings are followed over the long haul.

The destination we all long for is lasting, true love. As with any journey, if we want to arrive at our destination, we need to know where we've been, where we are now and where we want to go, and have an accurate map to guide us along the rest of the way. In the following chapters, we would like to help you look specifically at the map you've been using to get to where you are today in relationships and look at the trails you have been on. If you want to travel the road leading to a lasting relationship, you need to know whether the map you have will get you there. In other words, we ask ourselves, "Does my way of looking at love and the way I 'do' relationships have the potential to move me toward true love?"

PREPARATIONS
FOR THE JOURNEY

Chapter 3

Who Am I and
Where Have I Been?

Our relationship maps and guidebooks have been under development since we were children and reflect the sum of our instruction and experience in the area of male-female relationships. We usually don't take the time to think about what these maps look like, and when things don't go well in our love relationships, we often end up surprised and confused, thinking, "Hey, how did I end up here?"

Recently my son and I (Tom) went on a short mountain biking trip on a nearby trail. Our goal was to reach the summit of the mountain, which overlooks our town. Since we had never taken this trip before, we checked the trail map at the park headquarters and saw we needed to follow the trail with blue markings. It had recently rained, so we spent a fair amount of time dodging mud puddles, and after about an hour entered a segment of trail that became progressively narrower. We hadn't seen a blue marker for some time when my son, who was leading, yelled back, "Dad, look!" As I looked up from my present mud puddle, I saw we were next to someone's driveway on a road just a short distance from our house! Nonplussed, I asked the proverbial question: "How did we end up here?" As any typical thirteen-year-old would answer, my son responded, "You must have gotten us on the wrong trail." The more accurate answer was that we did not have a trail map with us, and I thought we could figure out the route as we went along. With all of the mud, washouts and other post-storm distractions, we simply lost our way.

That is a good description of what happens to many of us in relationships. Without an accurate map or guidebook to help us stay on track, it is easy to get lost. Each of us has developed our own version of a relationship guidebook that orients our journey of love. It consists of the beliefs and expectations we have for love relationships — a product of our life experiences that also includes our hopes and dreams for what our love relationships will become. If we are to create healthy, lasting relationships, we need to know what our guidebook tells us about ourselves, about what we expect from relationships and how both of these have been shaped by our life experiences to this point.

We invite you to consider three questions:

1. How do I see myself as a person?
2. What am I looking for in a love relationship?
3. How have my earlier life experiences influenced my expectations of love and relationships?

Understanding Ourselves

Think for a moment how you would respond to the question, "Who are you?" If our journey toward truly loving relationships is to be successful, it should begin with a clear answer to this question. Our first step is to understand ourselves as persons who have never been and will never be duplicated, as creations of God (assisted by our parents). As God's creations, we are made in his image and are, therefore, persons of infinite worth and dignity with the capacity for love. This human worth is the essence of our nature and is constant — it does not fluctuate from day to day.

Does your answer to "Who are you?" reflect this knowledge, or does your self-esteem — your opinion of your worth as a person — tell you otherwise? Your "self-esteem" can be a tremendous source of confusion on the journey when it is low in self-love. This is not a self-centered narcissism, but an honest self-acceptance of your own goodness rooted in God's unconditional love for you as an individual. Without self-acceptance, we can easily bypass the road to true love and wind up in an unending search for self-importance, power, pleasure, adequacy and acceptance from others. Certainly self-esteem rises and falls, and no one feels on top of his or her game all the time, but reaching our destination is in jeopardy if an internal belief in our personal worth is lacking.

The question, "Who am I?" can be followed by other questions such as "Do I like who I am?" "Do I appreciate myself?" "Do I take care of myself and respect myself?" and "Am I comfortable being alone?" If our answers are not "yes,"

or at least on the way to "yes," then we need to do some work. Reading and journaling, attending retreats and workshops or entering professional counseling or spiritual direction can all provide valuable assistance in improving our knowledge of ourselves as persons of worth and value, and in clarifying what we're looking for in a relationship.

Understanding Our Hopes for Love

Our initial hopes and dreams for love relationships often focus on how we long for another person to love us and how we'll feel when we're treated specially. We all have pictures in our heads (if not in our photo albums) of long walks, hugs, special notes and gifts, conversations, marriage, sexual intimacy and other images that come together to define a loving relationship. In fact, Gary Chapman in his book *The Five Love Languages* describes ways love can be communicated: quality time, acts of service, physical touch, words of love and giving gifts. Each of us, he says, has a primary language or two through which we hear the message that we are loved, and our "objectives" will reflect how we prefer to have that message communicated.[1]

It will be important for you to create a clear picture of how you hope your boyfriend, girlfriend, husband or wife will love you, but remember that true love is mutually affirming, so don't let your objective focus only on how someone will love you. True love requires that your focus be on ways you can love that fulfill another's dreams and help him or her become the most complete person he or she can become. Doing so will inevitably take you through times of disillusionment, disappointment and struggle, so expect the realities of challenge and growth alongside romantic hopes and dreams. Without the balance of the two, the temptation to travel the fast lane can become very strong. Our expectations for love are intricately tied to the things we learn about ourselves and relationships in our youth, so let's reflect on what these have been.

Understanding the Roots of Our Expectations

Our self-esteem and our expectations for love are rooted in our experiences in four areas:

- Family relationships: parents, relatives and siblings
- Social relationships: peers, school, neighborhood and work
- Media: TV, music, movies, books, Internet and magazines
- Church: religious education and formation, spiritual development

The interaction of these four areas develops our expectations and objectives for love relationships and provides the raw material from which our trail maps are made. More important, our experiences in these areas develop our beliefs and opinions about ourselves and mold our feelings of self-worth.

Family Relationships

The most critical influence in shaping our sense of identity is our family of origin. The ways in which we experience warmth or coldness, firmness or permissiveness, acceptance or rejection, affirmation or invalidation impact on our sense of self for a lifetime. While our parents certainly take the lead in this process, our siblings and other relatives also play a role. Many of us, for example, might have/had that special, unconditional loving relationship with a grandparent who helped us believe in our goodness no matter what storms of family life were brewing. Both of us

had grandmothers, for example, who only seemed to see us in one light: God's gift to them. The power of such affirmation is virtually matchless!

A useful concept in understanding the influence of family experience on our own love relationships is that of "core beliefs" or "schemas" identified by cognitive psychologists such as Dr. Judith Beck[2] and Dr. Jefferey Young.[3] Core beliefs are deeply rooted opinions that we have about ourselves that can take the form of "I am" statements. If, for example, I have grown up with loving parents in a relatively stable, supportive home that has positively met my needs, I'll likely conclude that I am competent, lovable and important. I'll have a stronger sense that I am good, I am safe and I am worthwhile and secure.

These beliefs will usually translate positively in love relationships outside my family. If, however, my family experiences have been damaging, neglectful and rejecting, I may conclude that I am inadequate, unlovable, unimportant, not good enough, vulnerable and worthless. These latter beliefs most often arise out of family dynamics in which a child learns to think this way because of being consistently treated in ways that send these messages. In other words, a child who is:

- neglected begins to believe he is unimportant;
- abused learns to think he is vulnerable;
- abandoned learns to think he is alone;
- harshly criticized learns to think he is inadequate;

- compared negatively to a sibling learns to think he is not good enough.

Often these connections are more noticeable in cases of severe family dysfunction, but it is important to realize that core conclusions can develop in the mind of any child in any family. In fact, it is very common to see these beliefs developing in the subtleties of family interactions without the presence of significant family dysfunction.

No child or growing adolescent wants to feel the anxiety, sadness, shame, guilt, hurt and anger triggered by such fears, so they attempt to figure out ways to keep the risks of experiencing these feelings to a minimum. Rules for how to think and act then develop in an attempt to keep the risks low.[4]

"I don't want to be abused and helpless, so I'll keep my feelings to myself and walk on eggshells."

"I don't want to be criticized and inadequate, so I'll be perfect and overachieve."

"I don't want to be neglected and unimportant, so I'll find someone to accept me."

"I don't want to be abandoned and alone, so I'll never let myself get close to anyone."

These rules become guidelines or reference points for assessing our own sense of worth and can direct many of our relationship decisions in an attempt to heal these wounds.

We Learn What We See

The second powerful influence on our love relationships is the lesson in love we see our parents model. Children learn more powerfully from what they see than from what

they are told. Last year, for example, we were having a run-
ning battle over our children's seeming inability to put their
backpacks away after school. They'd leave them anywhere
as they came in the house, generally in the middle of the
floor. One day, after racking our brains to figure out why
consequence after consequence didn't change their behavior, we spied our own briefcases plopped on a nearby bench!
It dawned on us that when we come home from work, our
briefcases drop wherever we come in! If modeling can impact our children in something as simple as backpack placement, it stands to reason that the way we treat one another
as husband and wife will have a massive impact on our
children's experience of love relationships.

Spend some time considering how your family has af-
fected your opinions of yourself and your worth, then list
the rules and expectations for love relationships that you've
seen modeled over the years. Where did your parents, step-
parents, guardians or significant others fall on these dimensions of relationship?

Respect---------------------------------- Disrespect

Building up ----------------------------- Cutting down

God as centerpiece --------------------- God as afterthought

Going each other's way ------------- Going separate ways

Shared decisions------------------------ Independent decisions

Joint finances --------------------------- Separate finances

Quality time with each other ------- No time with each other

Accepting differences ---------------- Pressure for conformity

Freedom -------------------------------- Possessiveness

Pride in accomplishments ---------- Jealousy

Self-giving ------------------------------ Self-centeredness

Open communication ---------------- Closed communication

Emotional expression ---------------- Emotional inhibition

Warmth --------------------------------- Coldness

Commitment --------------------------- Infidelity

Affirmation ----------------------------- Criticism

There can be many other themes to consider; try to identify any other modeling effects that may be significant in
the writing of your personal love relationship guidebook.
Many men and women, after starting positively on their
journey together, become horrified when they begin to have
the same kind of conflicts or difficult dynamics that their
parents did. This is actually to be expected since we never
really go through formal training in love relationships and
often have to rely on the ways we've seen it done before.

Social Relationships

By the time we are four or five years old, events occurring outside our families begin to have a greater impact on
how we look at ourselves and relationships. The dynamics
of our peer interactions can confirm or challenge our view
of ourselves, while the ways we observe our peers or other
adults interact continue to mold our beliefs about love.

Peers and self-esteem

Try to recall the early messages you received from your
peer relationships in general. Were you primarily accepted
and affirmed in ways that helped you feel positively about
yourself, or did you experience rejection and ostracism?
These experiences likely served to solidify your core feelings as either good, worthwhile and significant, or as not
good enough, worthless and unimportant. There is no
single formula, however, that translates social experiences

into self-beliefs because there are many intervening factors. The key is to understand how your experiences have
played out for you and influenced your relationship with
yourself and others.

Lessons in love

These social factors influencing your journey of love are
the specific lessons you received about relationships and
sexuality from parents, teachers and peers. Whereas parents are the primary educators of their children, generally
only ten percent of us would say that we learned about sexuality, love and relationships primarily from our parents. (If
you're in that ten percent, thank your parents...they have
given you a real gift!) Surveys we have taken during workshops and retreats document that most people credit their
friends and the media as their primary source of sexuality
information. Unfortunately, these sources are not always the
most desirable — or accurate.

In your life, where did you get your knowledge of sexuality and sexual matters, and how has it been incorporated
into your relationship map? In your family, was sex an open
topic or taboo? Were discussions about sexuality welcomed,
or were they sources of discomfort to be avoided? How have
these experiences influenced your ability to understand your
own sexuality and to talk about sexual feelings or issues?

Classroom contributions

In addition to your family's treatment of sexuality, consider the influences from any formal sex education training
received in school. If you're in your twenties or thirties, your
exposure to classroom sex education is probably very different from those in their forties or beyond, but that is not
necessarily all good news. What is good news is that some
sex education programs have become better at defining

sexuality as it relates to the whole person. Most programs now are acknowledging sexual feelings as a natural dimension of being human, which beats the messages we received in high school during the 1970s when, in religion class, we were given a book about sex in a brown paper bag!

What is not good, however, is that many sex ed programs cover sexual information without incorporating the context of values such as self-control, respect and chastity, which are prerequisites for reaching truly loving relationships. In other words, a message is presented to children as young as third or fourth grade that responsible sexuality means that you probably should wait to have sex until you are older and feel ready to handle it, but if you really "love" the person and don't wait, be sure to use a condom or some other form of "protection."

Think back to when you were in school and the things you were taught about love, sex and relationships. What values were you presented with (if any) that wrap around the sex information you received, and how do these values guide your actions today?

The talk on the street

How were your specific attitudes about love relationships influenced by your peers, especially through how they talked about and lived out heterosexual relationships? I (Tom) can remember many a weekend morning on the neighborhood basketball court during junior high school years listening to the high school kids bragging about their sexual exploits from the night before. After a few years with these guys, it was very clear in my mind that to be cool, with it and a real man, sexual involvement with a girl was the main measuring stick. More than that, the meaning of love was one-dimensional — it meant sex. That meaning, combined with other, "off the right trail" inputs such as pornography, led to a powerful equation: love = sex = self-worth, which became a really big reference point in my personal trail guide.

What reference points did you come away with from the years with your friends or other peer role models? What do you see in your current social circles? Are members of the opposite sex viewed or treated as persons to be respected in enjoyable friendships, or are they objects for pleasure and status? Which values and actions will move you toward truly loving relationships?

Media

Information and images obtained through various media outlets make up the third source of our love education. This conglomeration of attitude-shaping sources — televi-

sion, movies, books, magazines, newspapers, radio, CDs, the Internet and so on — is overwhelming in its volume, let alone impact. Media influences tell us what should be written in our relationship guides by providing us with images of what our relationship destinations should be and what it takes to get there. Unfortunately, for the most part, the past thirty years have quite radically altered the map of true love. Compare the image of love in TV comedies like "I Love Lucy" or "The Dick Van Dyke Show" to today's menu. A bit different, wouldn't you say?

It will be important for you to look at what you watch, read and listen to, and ask yourself what these tell you about love and relationships. Do they project and reinforce ideal values of fidelity, self-giving and unconditional and permanent commitment, or do they project self-centered enjoyment, fulfillment of needs, conditional acceptance and immediate gratification? Are persons loved for who they are and is love deep enough to hold persons together through challenging times, or are persons objects for one's desires — consciously or not?

If your experience is anything like ours, the scenes and images of sex or sexual innuendo you've viewed over the years number in the thousands, and most times are not between a husband and wife. In fact, most sexual encounters seem to occur within days of people becoming acquainted. Ask yourself, once again: Is what I am watching, listening to and reading helping me to move toward lasting relationships, or is it planting values and expectations within me that will lead me down other paths?

Church

A final source of training we should consider is that received from any religious institution or group. For many of us, this may be listed as "None" or "Not relevant," but we still need to know where spiritual components have come into play. You may have had positive influences from priests, ministers, rabbis, religious sisters and brothers, Sunday school, C.Y.O., youth groups, C.C.D. classes, retreats and so on. Such individuals and programs may have helped you to understand the beautiful person God created you to be and the unconditional love that God has for you. In addition, they would have been strong models of faith and lifelong commitment to the journey of love, helping you to develop values of kindness, goodness, forgiveness, acceptance, self-love and mutual respect. Realistically, however, this may not always have been the case, and it is important to ask ourselves, "Why not?" The most common answers are:

1. Religion was pushed on me by my parents, so I was turned off.

2. Religious role models were out of touch with reality, too interested in money, or they just personally turned me off.

3. Religious services were boring, and I never got anything relevant out of them.

4. Religious instruction was never able to help me understand how rules and spiritual principles related to everyday living.

5. Religion had too many "don'ts" that I didn't agree with and did not want to follow.

If these apply to you — or if you have others of your own — we hope that over time you can make some spiritual connections on a personal level in order to experience how these can support and nourish your journey of love.

Remember, we are made in the image and likeness of God and are trying to grow more fully into this image and likeness as we try to love the way God loves. The best way to get to know someone is to develop a close personal relationship with him or her, and so it is with God. If we want to love as God loves, we need to know God more intimately so we can know what it is like to be loved by him. A spiritual center of a strong relationship with God will serve as the foundation for a successful journey. So consider what messages you have received about love and relationships from your religious background. What messages have you received about yourself? What do's and don'ts have you heard about sex, love and relationships, and do you understand why religious tradition holds to them? Do you know God?

Once we understand how family, social, media and church-related sources of love education come together, we can take a closer look at whether our views, values, expectations and dreams for love can move us toward truly loving relationships. Has what we have learned been accurate and true, or has what we have learned led to misconceptions that will lead us down rough roads?

Chapter 4
Misconceptions of Love

We've seen how the educational influences of our family, friends, church and society have contributed to our conceptualizations of relationships. We now need to ask ourselves if these conceptualizations are right or wrong, helpful or hurtful. Are our images and visions of love accurate, healthy and capable of taking us toward lasting, true love, or do we have misconceptions of love that lead to misunderstandings of what love is really all about?

Let's focus on three broad misconceptions of love:

- Love is only a feeling.
- Love is sex.
- Love is security.

While all three are interrelated, it is helpful to look at each one individually.

Love Is Only a Feeling

Thinking that love is purely an emotion is the most common misconception of love. Feeling in love fills our senses with a dynamic joy, a leap of the heart and a rush of euphoria. As one young man put it, "When I'm in love, I could

36

dance in the clouds!" The
problem with this outlook is
that it defines love in only one
dimension: a feeling of happiness. Certainly, happiness
or feeling good is part of what
love is all about, and the feelings we experience are wonderful affirmations of the
fullness of life. We feel lifted
up, healed, accepted, cared
for and so on. Together we

laugh, we joke, we play, we dream, we talk, we listen...we
feel great. Even when we are sad and struggling in our individual lives, the acceptance and support from the one we
love can lead us to happiness and a sense of well-being.

In a lasting relationship, however, it is impossible to
"feel" this way all or even most of the time as struggle and
strain are the prerequisites for growth. Without growth, the
"feelings" grow stale and superficial and, after a while, happiness disappears. Under this misconception, love equals
happiness, and it becomes easy to conclude that if I'm not
happy, I'm not in love. This is one reason why so many
marriages end. One or both spouses believe that love equals
happiness, and when happiness is not experienced for a
while, resentment develops as one or both spouses think,
"You should be making me happy." These resentments further erode the relationship, often resulting in "happiness"
being sought elsewhere in work, addictions, affairs, sports
and so on.

Joe and Barb's three years of dating and courtship were
marvelously happy times...until they began planning their
wedding. Family pressures, expectations and money prob-

lems led to the first arguments they had ever had and some were huge blowouts. Walking down the aisle, Joe had major doubts about whether they should actually go through with their wedding. Eighteen months later, after increasingly more conflict and less and less happiness, they were divorced. Joe's reasoning, "We just didn't love each other any more." The real reason? Joe and Barb's misconception that love equaled happiness: "If we're not happy, we must not be in love. We're not happy; therefore we should split up and look somewhere else for happiness."

Love Is Sex

Misconception #2 is: love equals sex. Whether this misconception is rooted in our family, social environment or the media, it develops into the belief that love is measured by genital sexual pleasure and activity. The phrase "making love" has become so one-dimensional that for quite some time it has been interchangeable with "having sex." As a result, feeling loved becomes equated with feeling sexually satisfied.

Believing that love is sex inevitably leads to hurt, because the building blocks for true love (open communication, self-control, emotional intimacy, etc.) are not securely placed in the foundation of a relationship, so the relationship eventually crumbles. It is frightening just how common this misconception is. Some persons go through dozens of "love" relationships in which they interpret sex as a measure of love, and yet, having experienced hurtful endings to those relationships, never consider that love is much more than just sex.

Love Is Security

Many persons also believe that if they are truly in love, they will feel a sense of complete security, that is, a belief that life is good and they are okay because another person loves them. Love as security echoes that old saying, "He's got my whole world in his hands." In this misconception, the messages we receive via our relationship reassure us at a deep level, affirming that we are loved, wanted, special and not alone. The fear of being alone is a major threat to the security we want to feel and makes it quite easy for us to mistake the comforts of companionship for love. Many persons will even put up with all kinds of disrespect, mistreatment or abuse in order to avoid aloneness and say, time after time, "But I love her (him)."

Billy, for example, twice found evidence that Jaime, his fiancée, was cheating on him, but refused to confront her. Billy had been engaged once before and was too afraid to deal with this for fear of being alone "forever." The wedding happened and five years and two kids later, he filed for divorce. The reason? Jaime's marital infidelity.

The desire for security is a poor substitute for true love, and if combined with misconceptions of love as only a feeling or just sex, it becomes very difficult to live in lasting love.

Messing with Nature

The primary reason that misconceptions such as these take relationships off track is that they "mess around" with the natural order of human nature and love as God designed it. You're probably not going to hear that spoken about too often in today's media or at your local watering hole, but that is

the bottom line. Think about it. A central principle of God's design for love is not to use people as objects. People are to be treated with respect and honored as persons of infinite worth and dignity. Operating under the misconceptions we discussed sets the stage for people to be used or to use others because desires for pleasure, power or positive self-esteem are set at the center of one's attention, leading one to lose sight of the other as a person.

Remember in the Gospel of Matthew (4:1–11) when Satan tried to get Jesus to change the natural order or plan of God? First, Jesus was hungry after his forty days in the desert, so Satan suggested that Jesus turn the rocks into bread, enticing him with the pleasure of biological and emotional need fulfillment. Next, Satan offered Jesus the chance to show that he could act without consequences by jumping off the temple without getting hurt — a demonstration of power and control. Lastly, Satan enticed Jesus with the prestige and self-importance that would come with control over the kingdoms of the earth in exchange for bowing down to him. To each of Satan's attempts to change God's plan for Jesus and our redemption, Jesus responded in ways that affirmed the natural order of God and resisted Satan's temptations. Jesus had an objective understanding of God's design — that is, no misconceptions — and did not let any subjective needs or desires mislead him.

Understanding God's design for love requires us to have an objective picture of the way true love develops, especially if we hope to resist the temptations we will inevitably face on love's journey. That picture must go beyond the lessons we have had in our personal courses of love education and focus on the natural order through which true love is designed to move. Let's look at this natural progression of love more closely.

Chapter 5

The Dynamic Progression of Love

When we talk about dynamics in any field, we are referring to a process or a movement of energy. When we speak about the dynamics of love, we are talking about the ways love moves within us and between us and another person. This process is a natural, mysterious progression of emotion and action designed by God to bring us to both personal wholeness and lasting, truly loving relationships.

Perhaps one of the best descriptions of this process is that of Pope John Paul II in his work, *Love and Responsibility*.[5] He brings together for us five major pieces of love's puzzle that we must understand in order to solve the puzzle of love for our lives: the sexual urge, attraction, desire, goodwill and betrothed love.

The Sexual Urge

Understanding the dynamics of love begins by realizing that God has placed in us a sexual drive or "urge." This is a natural instinct to seek the opposite sex and try to find wholeness or completion of ourselves with another person. It is intrinsically a good thing because it is connected with God's work of creation. Our sexual urge or drive begins the process of conception — not just of a new human being, but also of a new human spirit. Our sexual urge serves the common good of society and is the starting point in the development of the dignity of persons. Human dignity cannot exist if the human person does not exist; hence our sexual urge keeps the process of creation alive.

We are most likely aware of our sexual urge in our quick reactions of attraction to others we see or meet, but we have to make a distinction between our sexual drive and sexual arousal. Most of us will feel aroused, for example, if we see a steamy bedroom scene in a movie, but it is not likely that we will think our desire for completeness as a person will be fulfilled by that actor or actress on the screen. Sexual stimuli will trigger sexual arousal — it is a very biological response. Although it involves sexual arousal, our sexual urge is more than a drive for sexual pleasure. It is a force that leads us out of ourselves and toward another.[6] It involves the inner life of each of us and reflects the divine working of God through which we can become co-creators of life.[7] This life is not just a "being," but a new spiritual, psychological, emotional, social and physical "person." As we partner with God in this creative process, we ourselves grow within to a new depth of spiritual, psychological, emotional, social and physical wholeness.

For this to happen, we have to be aware that our internal sexual urges are not separate from our free will and our ability to make conscious choices about how to externally respond to our sexual reactions.[8] If we don't exercise self-control and self-determination, personal enjoyment will become our primary focus and will begin to reduce another person to an object of that enjoyment. Each of us has to accept full responsibility for the way we live out our sexual urge because without this responsibility, the sexual behavior required for God's natural order of true love cannot exist. In Pope John Paul's words, the "urge is subordinate to the will."[9] Our sexual drive may be the basis from which love and joy will arise, but true love and true joy cannot exist without responsibility and self-control.

We usually don't think of the connection among love, joy and responsibility, but they are intimately linked. As Pope John Paul put it,

> There exists a joy that is consonant with both the nature of the sexual urge and with the dignity of persons. Joy results from collaboration, from mutual understanding and the realization of jointly chosen aims, in the broad field of action that is love between man and woman. Joy is bestowed by either great variety of pleasure connected with the differences of sex or by the sexual enjoyment that conjugal relationships can bring. God designed this joy and linked it with love between man and woman insofar that love dwells in a manner worthy of human persons.[10]

Attraction

Our sexual urge acts like a power cell that energizes our movement toward true love, with the first phase of that movement being the attraction we experience to another person. This attraction is, in a sense, Love 101 on the way to a Ph.D. Most of us could speak at length about what it feels like to be "attracted" to someone we meet: our eyes focus on that person and seem to drink in his or her appearance; our emotions are awakened in the jump of our hearts; butterflies swarm in our stomachs and energy buzzes through our brains, drawing us to that person. These reactions tell us clearly, "Hey! Here comes something good!"

On a more technical plane, our attraction is a composite celebration of sensory, cognitive, emotional and physiological circuits triggering a conscious or unconscious awareness that a person has entered our world who possesses qualities that may help us become whole and complete.[11] Just who we feel attracted to is a product of a long list of physical, hereditary and environmental factors, combined with whatever developments we have made in our sense of self over the years. The object of our attraction, for example, may have the warm eyes of our mother or a strength like our father. He or she may seem intelligent, handsome, athletic, soft, witty, beautiful, energetic or, in some other way, lead us to sense intuitively that he or she can add to our lives in some way. As a result, we feel the urge to "check that person out."

Our rush of attraction, which is driven by our sexual urge, is a sudden, terrifically pleasant and exciting feeling — but it is not always very reliable. These feelings are not overly concerned for or focused on the real person, since our eyes of attraction can see in someone qualities and traits that don't really exist.[12] Just as a slide projector can project an image onto a screen, we can project qualities we hope to see and possess onto that person standing in front of us.

Our relationships will have more substance if we make sure that we do not separate the qualities we are attracted to from that person as a whole. This is no easy task, as society urges us to target our attractions on shapely legs, sexy eyes, six-pack stomachs, tight butts and big breasts. If we look at a man or woman and keep our attractions focused only on his or her body, we lose sight of the whole person and set ourselves up for a shallow, utilitarian relationship. Such narrow attractions reflect the misconceptions of love, leading eventually to an empty feeling when that "good thing" we thought we found is gone.

Healthy love relationships require that we join our natural tendency to be drawn to certain dimensions of a person with the exercise of logic and reason in a way that broadens our focus to the whole person.[13] The deepening of our feelings for a person can then occur on a foundation of truth about that person, rather than on a foundation of infatuation and projection. "If attraction fastens first and foremost upon the value of the person versus various specific values, then attraction has the value of complete truth. The good to which attraction addresses itself is the person, not something else."[14] To quote an anonymous woman overheard in a restaurant bar, "I'm a person, not a pair of breasts."

Desire

The next step in the natural dynamics of love is desire — the desire for our sense of self to be completed by another.[15] This need takes us beyond our initial attraction and begins to unite us in relationship. Desire in this context is more than mere sensual desire — a self-interested infatuation and quest for fun, pleasure or avoidance of pain. The desire we're talking about is more of a "completion desire" — a true longing for that person to be a part of our lives and a part of ourselves. The true dynamic of this desire is that it values the worth and dignity of the other person. The man or woman we desire is not an object made up of qualities we need to feel happy. He or she is a person to relate to, to grow with and to connect with, not just someone to take from.

Experience tells us that the dynamics of desire begin to capture our awareness anywhere from several days to several weeks after meeting someone. By this time, our guy or girl is on our mind almost constantly; we feel a flutter when we think about seeing each other or talking on the phone and we ponder such questions as, "I wonder if she likes me?" or "Could he be the one?"

At this point, our learned relationship expectations and guidelines shape the way we handle our desire and take us to a crossroads. One road leads to "True Love," the other road takes us to a dead end. If we believe that love is just emotion, sex and security, then heading into the dead end is a pretty sure bet. Just like the 1991 North Atlantic "perfect storm," when three vigorous sources of energy collide, it's impossible to get where you want to go. Bringing together the three misconceptions that love is only emotion, sex and security guarantees we won't get very far as we become overwhelmed and confused by huge waves of "that feeling."

Oh, What a Feeling!

"That feeling" was best summed up for us by Sam, a woman in her early twenties who had been dating a man about a month. Sam had a difficult childhood marked by her parents' divorce and her father's alcoholism. She had also recently experienced the breakup of a three-year relationship with a man with whom she had been engaged and sexually involved. Following the breakup, she feared that she would never find another man to love her, because she must be unlovable and worthless. The first four weeks of this new relationship were very intense with attraction, and Sam's head was spinning as she tried to decide which way to go in the relationship. Following one romantic evening, Sam was at a crossroads and described it this way: "When he kissed me on the neck and whispered in my ear, 'I think you're wonderful,' I walked away overcome by that feeling." For Sam, the joy of emotion, the sexual arousal and the affirmation that she was lovable and worthwhile collided to form that feeling. It was that feeling which led Sam to believe that she was in love and had her seriously consider moving in with her new boyfriend.

In reality, that feeling was "completion" desire. It was, however, desire misshapen by lessons of life that produced a belief that wholeness is defined as happiness, closeness and security arrived at by means of a relationship. Those lessons, unfortunately, would take her in the wrong direction in her quest for lasting, true love, most likely bringing her to a repeat of the relationship she had ended six months earlier. The whirling winds of desire, urged her, as they can for all of us, to leap into love before she could really know the truth about who her boyfriend was. Sam was focused more on her own needs, and projected qualities onto him that mainly reflected her own wish for completion, especially her hope that he could make her feel worthwhile, lovable and secure.

Sam's feeling was rooted in her desire and told her, "Feels good, must be love, go for it." The road to true love is, in fact, rooted in desire, but requires a level of self-con-

trol that says, "Feels good, might be love, start with friendship."

Goodwill and Friendship

Whether Sam, you or me, the pushes and pulls of desire
are all part of the healthy, natural order of God's design for
love. For love to be true, we must move beyond love as desire and long for what is best for our girlfriend or boyfriend,
not just what is best for ourselves. This is the essence of
love as "goodwill" — to willingly seek what is good for another without any self-centered ulterior motive. To love in
this way will certainly help us move toward our own fulfillment, but goodwill by its nature gives unconditionally.[16]
Goodwill journeys beyond the thought of what we can get
out of our giving. Desire will always stay an energy between us, but we have to take our God-given will-power
and prevent desire from dictating the course of the relationship and limit how completely we can come to know
this person we love.[17]

Friendship

Ultimately, the development of goodwill in a relationship allows friendship to become a reality. Friendship is first
realized when we are aware that our love is moving us from
two "I's" to a "we." A true friendship can only happen if
the two of us make a free-will choice to mutually give our
hearts to each other. This is not yet a commitment to the
point of a betrothed, forever love, but it is on a level of a
fully reciprocal concern and compassion. In other words, in
friendship, love is a decision in which the attraction, desire
and emotion I feel for you is directed toward your well-
being as a person, while your attraction, desire and emotion is simultaneously directed toward my well-being.[18] This

decision is love as goodwill. Friendship, then, is "a full commitment of the will to another person with a view toward that person's good."[19]

True love, therefore, is not just an outlet for your feelings, a sexual release or an infusion of belief in your own value and security. True love involves a transformation of that feeling into a friendship that allows both of you to enjoy each other through deeper experiences that affirm each other as persons.[20] This is not enjoyment expressed as pleasure, which sends us each the message that "I'm using you as an object." Pleasure of itself will not create a lasting bond and can lead the two of you to stay united only so long as the pleasure lasts. That feeling, however, when transformed through goodwill sends a very different, powerful message: "I respect and value you as the person you are and will not use you as a tool for my own enjoyment, pleasure or comfort." This respect allows us to trust one another and find the peace and joy in our friendship that can't be found if one or both of us know we have a more self-centered agenda.

The recipe for this depth of respect, trust and love calls for a major ingredient: time. Knowing someone well enough to risk putting trust in his or her goodwill for you simply can't happen quickly. It literally takes months, probably years, to achieve. In Sam's case, the level of relationship she wanted after one month was impossible, since she and her new boyfriend hadn't even become friends yet, let alone pseudo-spouses.

Betrothed Love

If we choose to practice the self-control and patience necessary to create goodwill and friendship, then our journey of love can move toward its deepest dimension: the full giving of ourselves to our friend in betrothed love. This state of love is more than working for what is good for someone else — it is more than a good friendship. Betrothed love is surrendering ourselves to the man or woman we love with a will that is ready and able to commit itself to the service of that person's growth. Betrothed love is a self-sacrificing love that nurtures the other's growth toward fulfillment and ultimately toward God. This depth of love is a synergy of attraction, desire, goodwill and friendship that moves beyond these levels to a fully mutual sharing of one's soul with the other.[21]

The self-surrender of betrothed love has to be equally committed to by both and lived daily in ways that create a "perfect whole." We experience such wholeness only when there is a unity of the spiritual, psychological, emotional, social and physical parts of ourselves with the spiritual, psychological, emotional, social and physical life of our beloved. This union embraces our sexuality — our entire identity — and is way beyond mere physical sexual intimacy. The unitive process is actually quite paradoxical because as "I" surrender myself to you, "I" don't disappear or become your slave. "I" am, instead, enlarged, enriched and fulfilled in return.[22] The power of this self-surrendering love finds its physical expression in marital intercourse, which further intensifies the bond of unity between a couple and must be totally exclusive: it cannot be given to more than one person.[23]

Is Surrender a Good Thing?

It's not surprising to find our heads spinning as we try to make sense of all this. We remember how hard it was to grasp this the first or second (tenth?) time around, especially that term *self-surrender*. What's that about, anyway?

Since a full discussion of this concept is beyond the scope of this book, it may be best to think of it as a choice to "give life" to our beloved. When a woman, for example, gives life to a child, she offers the nurturing environment of her womb to that growing baby, and hopefully works hard at good prenatal health in order to give that baby the best shot he or she can have at growing into a healthy human being. This mother does all of this unconditionally, without expecting anything in return from that child. In other words, she has surrendered herself to her baby. In the process, she does not lose her identity, but instead grows in her own maturity, fullness and wholeness within herself.

The self-surrender of betrothed love is similar to this. We unconditionally give life to our beloved by consciously choosing to act in ways that provide nourishment, security and growth, regardless of whether the current stretch of the journey is smooth or rocky. When such a commitment is lived out by both of us in a daily decision to love, our self-surrender to one another creates a relationship that is mutually nourishing, supportive and secure.

The Actions of True Love

We had said earlier that, ultimately, true love is loving someone the way God loves — completely, unconditionally and permanently. To be able to love in this way, we have to do certain things and act in certain ways in order to give life to the one we love. The best summary of love as action is 1 Corinthians 13:

"Love is patient, love is kind, it isn't jealous, doesn't boast, isn't arrogant. Love is not dishonorable, isn't selfish, isn't irritable, doesn't keep a record of past wrongs. Love doesn't rejoice at injustice but rejoices in the truth. Love endures all things, love has complete faith and steadfast hope, love bears with everything. Love never ends" (1 Cor 13:4–8).

In truth, we don't love in these ways all of the time. We can be impatient and sarcastic, jealous, envious, conceited, stuck-up, arrogant, selfish, rude, demanding, irritable, resentful and unforgiving. Depending on our mood, we can jump on each other in a flash, snicker when the other gets hurt and get defensive or sulk when we're proven wrong. We can calculate a huge tally of debts to be repaid for our loyalty, we can doubt one another, we can lose faith in each other and retreat when the other is under stress. Sounds like a great relationship, doesn't it?

During times when such hurtful experiences bring struggle to our relationship, St. Paul's words can remind us that we have a choice. We can either keep choosing to be self-centered or choose to surrender ourselves to the love to which we have committed — a betrothed love that puts ego aside and attempts to give life to each other and our relationship. To do this we must drop our guard, open our hearts and look at the wisdom St. Paul provides and do as he says:

BE PATIENT: We have all heard that patience is a virtue. True love absolutely requires patience. Few of us find it easy to wait for what we want, but impatience in relationships quickly leads to actions that invalidate someone's worth and sets the stage for feeling used.

BE KIND: Kindness is required for good communication in our relationships. It affirms our appreciation and love for our beloved. If we choose sarcasm, criticism, harsh judgment and the like, love can wither faster than a rosebush in a drought.

BE HUMBLE: Do any of us like to be with people who strut their stuff, think they're "all that" and tell us so? No. Conceit, big-headedness, grandiosity or exaggerated self-

importance makes us very tough to communicate with and often leads to feelings of vulnerability and dissatisfaction in relationships, especially when the other person is ready to grow and mature. Choosing to be humble and modest sets the stage for patience and kindness that, in turn, promote humility. Humility is not a submissiveness that leads to being walked on in a relationship. Instead, humility is a confident belief in the goodness and truth about ourselves as persons of dignity, which allows us to value ourselves and set healthy relationship boundaries.

BE GENEROUS: The willingness to give time, service, loving words, touch and so on, especially when we're not feeling so inclined, becomes true acts of charity that nurture a relationship. Without such nourishment, one easily becomes hardened in arrogance, selfishness and rudeness, things that suck the life out of any relationship.

BE GENTLE: Irritability, resentment and anger likely cause more tension within ourselves and in relationships than any other emotion. We need to find ways of consciously managing these emotions, so that the way we act on and talk about these feelings can allow us to be gentle with one another. If we can, the gentleness with which we share ourselves with one another will almost always soften our hearts and bring us back into a loving focus.

BE JUST: In what can be one of the more humorous ways of giving life and surrendering to betrothed love, we have to be open to justice in our relationships. (Have you ever thought about how funny we can look trying to defend a position we know is wrong?) We need to be fair, honest and willing to say we're wrong when we're wrong without defensiveness. If love rejoices in the truth, being just also means accepting the truth of who we are as persons, and not demanding that someone else be simply who we think he or she should be.

BE FAITHFUL: We can only have one person to whom we can be betrothed in love. If our love is true, it requires that we be faithful to that person. We most often think this applies in a sexual realm. Yet faithfulness and loyalty also must be present in other ways such as being dependable, trustworthy, trusting, respectful to each other in public as well as in private and so on.

BE PERSEVERING: Don't give up. Anything worth having is worth the work.

BE FORGIVING: Intertwined among all of St. Paul's statements of what love is and isn't, we can see the necessity for forgiveness. Love challenges us to forgive one another by asking for forgiveness, offering forgiveness and accepting forgiveness. Unfortunately, we often hurt the people we love and they hurt us, so without forgiveness, it is virtually impossible to follow true love's path.

Each of these actions, while certainly not sole properties of betrothed love, needs to be part of how we love each other if the complete, unconditional and permanent possibilities of true love are to be realized. We all fall short of these standards — we are human — but in betrothed love, we are to be like the phoenix and rise up out of the ashes of disillusionment by surrendering ourselves to the greater good of our relationship and to the growth and goodness of the one we love. At these times, we can only do so if we accept that love is a verb — an action word that is more than emotion, sex and security, and that our only path is to recommit to God's design of true love.

The Bible gives us many examples of people who have integrated the principles of betrothed love, none greater than Jesus and his mother, Mary. In the Garden of Gethsemane, Jesus chose to recommit to the path God had laid out for him and demonstrated the complete, unconditional and permanent love of God for us by surrendering to the way of the cross.

Mary, although young and unsure of what the future held, surrendered herself to God's plan for her to be the mother of Jesus. She gave herself completely, unconditionally and permanently to a life of love that brought both intense joy and pain along with it. For both Mary and her Son, love was a verb — a call to action, decision and commitment.

A Breather

Did you ever have a teacher in school who gave the classic assignment to write one paragraph describing your entire summer vacation? We know our usual reaction was, "No way can I get all that into one paragraph!" Echoing those sentiments, no way can we get every important dimension of the dynamics of love into one chapter. Realistically, we hope that you can hold this information against your present conceptions of love and evaluate where you stand in your awareness of God's design for love. Only when we understand that true love's natural order is drawn by our sexual urge through attraction, desire and friendship to betrothed love can we continue to grow in God's image and likeness — to love as God loves. Unfortunately, our world has disrupted the natural flow to the point where it is often hard to recognize it, let alone trust in it. As a result, we can become very susceptible to temptations of pleasure, power and prestige and follow their pull far away from true love. It is quite likely that you, like us, have experienced this pull and possibly ended up on many wrong trails.

If we have the right trail map — the natural order of love — where do we find lasting and true love? How does it happen? We've looked so far at who we are as persons — that is, what we are looking for in relationships — and at where we have been in our education in love. The next step in figuring out how we can make true love a reality is to look at the way we've lived out our relationships or the way we think we ought to live them out. Our experiences of love, sex and sexuality continue to shape our journey and, through our "on-the-job training," give us ongoing opportunities to evaluate what works and what does not work in developing lasting relationships.

EXPERIENCING
THE JOURNEY

Chapter 6

Experiences and Reference Points

Our Experience of Love

The ways we navigate relationships are rooted in our family and social stories and grow through various developmental stages, but on a practical level, how does a lasting love really come about?

We can help frame our answer to this question by asking a similar one in the context of career success: "How does a lasting, fulfilling career come to be?" While there are, as always, countless individual paths, most of us usually begin our work lives while finishing our education. We are comparatively immature and filled with preconceived notions regarding the "world of work." We choose our first job (or it finds us), often with limited actual experience or hands-on knowledge of the workplace, while relying on feedback from family members, mentors, role models and peers. We look for a decent match between what we think we'd like to do, what we're good at and what is available, although not necessarily in that order.

My (Tom's) first job as a psychologist, for example, was at a school in Mastic Beach, New York. I had finished most of my education and heard from a supervisor at my internship placement that a position was open. I needed the money, so without much soul-searching, I applied and was hired. It was not an ideal job, but it was a place to start.

Our first jobs often open doors to different jobs and, as we gain experience in our field, we learn about the realities of the workplace. We begin to adjust our expectations and assumptions and look for the things we believe we need for a "satisfying" career. A career journey most often will take us on one of three roads. We may stay within the same profession we were trained for, changing jobs and responsibilities as we grow and mature, or we may change professions until we find one that clicks for us. In the latter case, we're still growing and maturing, but we apply our lessons of experience to a different field than the one we started in, although it may be related. The third road heads in the opposite direction and is the path of the "unsatisfying" career, which is marked by frequent job loss or change without a sense of direction, purpose or insight into why things are not working out.

Most of our relationship journeys exhibit a flow of experience similar to one of these three career patterns. Our first love relationship is usually heavily influenced by assumptions arising out of our family and social love education. The person we were involved with was likely someone in our then current social, school or work circles to whom we initially related through a fair number of preconceived notions. Whether we had subsequent relationships or stayed with our first love, our relationships should show a growth and maturation in assumptions, expectations and actions toward more realistic understandings and abilities to create a lasting love. Unfortunately, however, some of our history shows, instead, a string of unsatisfying relationships marked by frequent relationship changes without a sense of direction, purpose or insight into why things are not working out.

Reference Points

As we look at our relationship experiences, we can observe the workings or internal guidelines for our love relationships. These guidelines serve, in a sense, as our relationship "reference points," or those conscious and unconscious expectations, assumptions, beliefs and values that steer our actions and guide our relationship decisions. The development of relationship principles and guidelines began during the early years of our love education and are continually refined and rewritten as we move through our experiences of love.

An Examination of Relationship Conscience

Take some time to review your relationship experiences and look honestly at the ways you have developed them. You may wish to evaluate your experiences according to the developmental stages of love and ask yourself the following questions for each relationship:

Attraction

Where did we meet?

What did I find attractive in his or her appearance, personality and way of relating to me and to others?

Did I initially see him or her as a person or just a body?

Did I truly want to get to know him or her, or was I hoping to get something from him or her (e.g., sex, stature, attention, companionship, etc.)?

How urgent was my "need" to get to know him or her?

Desire

How long after we met did we start talking/dating?

How much time did we spend together each day, week and so on?

How often and for how long did we talk on the phone, e-mail or use Instant Messenger?

What did we enjoy doing together?

How did I treat him or her?

What did I like/dislike about how he or she treated me?

What messages did the way I was treated send me about myself: for example, I am special, lovable, wanted, important?

Why were these messages important to me?

How was my self-esteem influenced by our relationship?

Did I feel infatuated and, if so, when did I start to feel it?

Did I feel a longing for him or her — a desire for completeness?

When did I think I was "in love"?

How did I define love?

Goodwill and Friendship

Were we compatible?

How did I communicate? How well did I listen and share my thoughts, feelings, needs and desires?

Did I feel his or her well-being was my priority?

Did I feel sexual desire for him or her and, if so, how did I respond to it?

Did we do any hand-holding, hugging, cuddling, light kissing or French kissing?

Did we engage in any petting or genital fondling, mutual masturbation, oral or anal sex or sexual intercourse? If so, when did it begin and how often did it occur? How important was it to the relationship and me? Was I comfortable with it?

Did we live together without being married?

How did I handle frustration, disillusionment and disappointment in our relationship?

Betrothed Love

Did we reach a depth of betrothed love?

Did I surrender myself to him or her and was it mutual?

Did I commit myself to his or her growth as a person?

Did we get engaged?

Did we get married?

Has our love lasted? If not, why not?

When Love Didn't Last

When did I realize that the relationship was becoming difficult?

Was there verbal, physical or sexual abuse?

Was there any substance abuse involved in the relationship?

How did I respond to our difficulties?

If the relationship ended, who ended it and how did I deal with it?

How did I feel after it was over?

How long was it before I started a new relationship?

Looking at your experience, summarize your relationship reference points. What assumptions, expectations, guidelines and so forth, were you operating under and how did they affect your actions? Perhaps the best question to ask yourself is, "Why did I do that?" or "Why was that important to me?" We hope you will focus on your experiences of relationships as you develop these answers, since they are central to answering our main question: "How does lasting, true love come to be?" In doing so, we suggest you look at the ways you have lived out your relationships along with the assumptions that support your actions. As you do, compare your guidelines to the broad guidelines and principles of healthy relationships that we will identify along the way.

This part of our discussion becomes more difficult since you assume the role of author for your own experiences. As you read on, be assured that our description of reference points for lasting relationships is not intended to pass judgment in any way. We don't know anyone, ourselves included, who has loved completely according to the "book" — God's, that is. We all fall short in some way or another. Each of us is asked to judge our own actions in order to personally assess if we are on the best road to truly loving and lasting relationships. Keeping this perspective in mind, let's examine our experiences as they occur over the different phases of love and relationships.

Chapter 7

Relationship Beginnings and Boundaries

Our Attraction Reactions

Having described what attraction is, let's focus on where it happens, what form it takes and what we do with it. Attraction brings us to the doorway of the relationship production studio where the potential drama and mystery of a human relationship is about to begin and we, in a sense, are the directors.

"Lights!"

When the call for "lights!" is heard on a movie set, the background is illuminated and all eyes focus on the subjects of the story about to unfold. If the set isn't just right, the script is hard to follow. In what settings have your relationships begun? Where do you expect to begin a relationship with the man or woman of your dreams?

Too often, our reference points for beginning relationships pay little attention to *where* they actually start. All of us would like to meet Mr. or Ms. Right, but get caught in a peculiar reasoning process. We think, "Where can I meet single people my age who share my interests and values?" instead of asking, "Where can I meet people who share my interests and values who are single and my age?" The first perspective frequently takes us to bars, clubs, parties or some other relationship marketplace, while the latter takes us to places that are interesting and fulfilling to us as individuals, and does not put us directly in a relationship hunt.

In speaking to several single men and women one day about what qualities they hoped to find in a boyfriend/girlfriend, all identified traits such as sincerity, honesty and trustworthiness. When asked for a general personality description of the kind of person they would most often meet in a bar or club, they responded quickly and unanimously: "players" — people who are more interested in what they can get than in a sincere relationship. So why go to bars to meet people? Their response: "Where else can you find them?" Can you catch the problem with the logic here?

One of these women said that all guys aren't players so she would take her chances. Undoubtedly, there are good people out on the club circuit and some wonderful relationships have actually begun in bars, but consider this for a moment: just because all of the inhabitants of the Amazon River aren't piranhas, water snakes and crocodiles, it doesn't mean I'm going to jump in for a swim. No matter how much I hope to meet a "nice" fish, I'd prefer to avoid the risk and find somewhere else to take a dip.

An alternative way to meet people is to pursue our interests in life — education, careers, volunteer work, spiritual enrichment, hobbies, enjoyable activities and so on, and, since we will be crossing paths with other people with similar interests, allow relationships to grow from the natural interactions with others in these settings. Such settings should not have alcohol or drugs as the medium of interaction. Meeting people under the influence is not the best way to begin a relationship — we're not the real us and they are not the real them. In any event, we need to trust that, as in all things, God has a relationship plan for us and, if meant to be, it will happen in his time, not necessarily in ours.

What about personal ads and the Internet? Although there are always exceptions — a couple we know met through a personal ad and have a wonderful relationship — personals are risky and we do not recommend them as a reference point for starting relationships. The same principle applies to the Internet. In both arenas it is tempting to present oneself in a less than authentic way. There is no good substitute for meeting people face-to-face in the day-to-day circles of life.

"Camera!"

When the lights of attraction go up, the camera of our mind focuses on that person before us. Whether it's a first meeting or the first realization that an attraction exists, the camera of our mind switches on and begins to record an initial "map" of that person's body, personality and spirit.

Regardless of when it happens, our initial attractions usually focus on another's physical appearance, although personality, way of carrying oneself or the aura of who one is in general can also be part of our initial focus. Focusing is usually not a conscious process, just a total reflex.

Think about the image of a person you are or would be attracted to, and what it is about him or her that draws your focus. This helps frame the reference points needed for the way you respond to those attractions.

"Action!"

Once we become aware of our initial attraction, we become responsible for how we choose to respond. One choice is to zero in on whatever physical, social or personality characteristics initially attracted us, and either pursue him or her for physical pleasure and emotional satisfaction, or obsess about him or her from afar. A second response would be to look beyond superficial characteristics to discover the person as a whole, and either engage him or her in conversation or admire him or her from afar. Seeing the person as a person and talking to him or her is the best relationship beginning, but isn't always easy to achieve. Thoughts of a warm embrace, a passionate kiss, a sexual encounter, a prize on your arm and the like are easy routes for our minds to travel given pervading cultural pressures. How can we see, for example, a woman-person and not a pair of breasts, or a man-person and not a cute butt?

First, we have to acknowledge that it is possible — and preferable — to see an individual as not just a body, but as a unique person. Next, since this doesn't always come naturally, we have to practice exercising our will to keep our thinking in the right direction. This works best if you have something you can say to yourself in the midst of an attraction reaction, such as, "Look at his (her) eyes, a whole person is in there," or "She's (he's) a person, not an object," or "I wonder what God's plan for him (her) is?"

Another way is to think for a minute how that person may have looked as a child. This sometimes helps to give us a view of a person in the process of becoming instead of a body for our using. Lastly, if our experience in attraction mode is a sense of urgency to get to know this man or woman, we need to take a deep breath and think about what is driving this urgency. Remember, fireworks fizzle, candles linger.

The Boundaries of Desire

Once we've met and our initial attraction has led us through our first moments (maybe hours) together, we begin to feel that growing desire to be together, and our reference points, expectations and beliefs about how a relationship should progress start to kick in. As these direct our pursuit of love, we become captivated by our desire for wholeness and start to set boundaries around that desire.

Boundaries are the guidelines or parameters that we use to structure relationship components like the time we spend together, the depth of conversation, physical contact, emotional closeness and so on. Boundaries are products of our education and experience and act as a behavioral foundation upon which the rest of the relationship will be built. Just as with any other construction process, a lasting structure depends on a firm foundation, but how will we construct it? Will we use solid building techniques, or will we take some cheap shortcuts?

Time Together

How much time have you spent with someone after meeting him or her? How often did you talk on the phone, write letters or e-mail, go out on dates and so forth? The amount of time that we try to spend together often reflects the strength of our desire for wholeness. We can experience problems early on if our time boundaries are set in ways that allow so much time together that undue pressure is put on the relationship. It can be like trying to frost a cake before it's baked. Many of us can relate to the idea of being "smothered" in a relationship or being a "smother-er." While sometimes such attention can be flattering or, at least, tolerated in the beginning, such intensity is seldom healthy down the road.

For now, a reference point that seems to work best is setting time boundaries that permit both people their own space, yet allow for a gradual entry into this new relationship. Restrain yourself from becoming all consumed with this new person, since doing so makes it harder for the relationship to follow love's natural progression. Our initial attractions and desires to be together can certainly be very intense. It is challenging to proceed with caution. If we move too quickly the foundation necessary to fully support our desire for wholeness does not have enough time to set, and we risk developing cracks in that foundation that may well cause the relationship to crumble.

But You Make Me Feel So Good!

Our core beliefs — those deep opinions of our personal worth, value and adequacy — are powerful motivations for wholeness and completion that serve as pivotal reference points for setting relationship boundaries. We get a picture of these at work when we find the connections between the way we are treated in our relationship and the way we feel about ourselves. The flavor of our time spent together and the types of things we do with one another send us important messages that impact our self-esteem. If the way we're treated sends a message that affirms us (e.g., "You are special"), that message is well received and we respond with wholeness — seeking reactions that usually keep us coming back for more. When we are treated in a way that tells us we are loved, wanted or special, we will usually be drawn to that person. His or her interest in us, desire to spend time with us, touching us, listening and sharing thoughts and feelings or doing nice things for us are incredibly affirming boosts to our sense of self-worth.

As always, our risk for relationship burnout increases when our desires are so strong that we quickly become dependent on these core affirmations, which sets us up to be hurt. A frequent indicator that such a dependency may be in the making is the "Swear-u-ben" relationship. This question — "So where have you been?" — is usually asked by our friends who haven't seen us very much over the past several months because we've been spending all of our time with our new boyfriend or girlfriend, to the exclusion of spending any time in previously enjoyed activities.

The road to lasting love is better paved with balance between time spent in relationship and time spent in other aspects or interests of life. We have to allow ourselves enough time to get to know the real person who has become the focus of our desires in order to be sure that he or she is not just on their best behavior until an agenda is obtained. Getting together once or twice a week for the first several months of a relationship is a good guideline for maintaining balance.

In any event, our desire to move deeper into this new relationship is driven by the emotional high we feel along with the excitement of what lies ahead. Soon, we start to think, "I think I'm in love!" But am I?

Chapter 8
Am I in Love?

In your relationship experience, how long was it before you first thought that you were in love? How long would you expect it to take? Are you the type of person who sees somebody across the room and thinks, "That's her, she's the one for me," or are you the individual who, after years of dating, still asks, "Do I truly love her?" A different question may be more accurate: "Am I in love, or am I infatuated?"

Infatuation

Remember Sam? She was a spokesperson for "that feeling" back in chapter 5, and was clearly experiencing infatuation: excitement and intense attraction dressed in an urgency to spend as much time as possible with her new guy. Most of us have experienced infatuation, which is normal and natural. God wired an infatuation circuit into our brains as part of our sexual urge, so being infatuated with someone is not a bad thing in itself. According to Fr. William Bausch, infatuation "is a hormone-induced, short-term, in-love high. The attraction, the feelings, the pulse are warm and wonderful, painful and wild."[1] Can't say it any better than that!

The operative word here is *short-term*. Infatuation is, in a nutshell, short-lived passion. Psychologists, philosophers and authors use the word *infatuation* with others like foolish, illogical and unreasoning. Yet even though these may be appropriate modifiers, we infatuateds are usually experiencing too much fun and fulfillment to allow such negative thoughts to slow us down. Our senses, hopes and dreams are saturated with our guy or girl, and since often reciprocated, infatuation invites both of us to indulge in deeper and deeper experiences of each other. Doing so, we extend the emotional and physical boundaries of our relationship. Keeping that feeling alive becomes our priority and can create marvelous opportunities for affirmation. But…is this love?

Words of Love

One difficulty we face in trying to discern if we're "in love" is that the word *love* is so broadly used. In some way, "love" is in the same semantic boat as "snow." In nonarctic climates, we identify anything white falling from the sky by one name: snow. Unlike we warm-airs, folks in Alaska or other arctic areas have more than a dozen words for the various types of white stuff. They don't overgeneralize.

When it comes to the word *love,* we definitely overgeneralize! We place it in so many different contexts that its meaning can easily become clouded. Similar to prescription medications, it's as if love has become a generic term allowed as an acceptable substitute for a multitude of specific emotions and experiences.

How do *you* define love? Take a minute to answer, then check if your definition is reflected in any of these headlines:

Couple celebrating fifty years of marriage vows says, "Our love will last forever."

Woman leaves husband of fifty years for a thirty-three-year-old guy and says, "I just don't love him anymore."

Another fatal attraction — man kills girlfriend's husband for love.

Coeds making love more than ever!

Husband refuses to split from demeaning, controlling wife: "I hate her but I love her."

Actor caught in love triangle.

"Love" is defined as commitment, fulfillment, adultery, sexual intercourse, dependency, care, enjoyment and so on, not to mention the many other ways we use the word to describe pleasure of some kind: "I love chocolate," "I loved that show," "You'll love this car" and on and on. As author John Kippley wrote, "The word 'love'...has degenerated to mean something someone may like to do because it might make him or her feel good in doing it."[2]

The line between infatuation and love, then, is often quite fuzzy. We need some way of describing our feelings, thoughts and actions over the course of a relationship that can help us better understand where we are in our experiences of love, especially when we are infatuated. We need a guide or compass with clear directional points.

We — your authors — met at Fairfield University in Connecticut and after several months of being distant acquaintances, began to feel an attraction to each other while attending a campus self-defense course. Tom (the instructor) was impressed with Donna's (the student) side thrust kick, and Donna was struck by Tom's ability to count in Korean and look good in a white dobok. Being somewhat on the "take it slow" trail, it wasn't until three or four months later when classes ended and we were back home in separate states that emotions were in full swing. By then our budding relationship was marked by long phone calls, long letters (no e-mail back then) and fun-filled weekend activities. "That feeling" was intense and alive, but was it love or infatuation?

Infatuation versus Love

It was infatuation. Our actions toward one another were certainly loving demonstrations of gentleness, generosity, kindness, fun and affirmation, but we were totally immersed in the present with little awareness of where each of us really had been in life and where we were going. This focus on the here and now is, perhaps, the clearest criterion to use in discerning the difference between infatuation and love, especially true love. When we're infatuated, we are totally focused on the present — the emotions, the sensations, the joys, the highs — all flowing through the attraction and desire dimensions of love's progression. In fact, we often become so focused that we become stuck there — at least for a while.

Infatuation is a comfortable time of smooth sailing in our relationship, during which we set our sights on the qualities we see in each other that can bring us toward completion and wholeness. It can become a difficult time, however, if we set our sights only on our own desires for pleasure. Either way, without progression to the deeper levels of love, infatuation begins to erode the relationship.

Falling in Love

This is a good time to examine that old phrase, "Falling in love." It certainly is one of the most common ways we describe our emotional reactions in the early part of a relationship. We encourage you to consider that "falling in love" is actually a misnomer. "Falling" reflects a loss of control caused by the pull of gravity when balance is lost. "Falling" is outside the realm of free will. We may fall into attraction and desire or tumble into infatuation, but it is much more accurate to say, "I'm walking toward love," or "I may be heading toward love." How can we know if we are, in fact, heading in the right direction?

Chapter 9

Compatibility, Communication and Closeness

A Relationship Compass

In the earlier phases of past relationships, what compass have you used to figure out if you were heading toward a lasting, truly loving relationship? Often, we simply ask ourselves the "Am-I-in-love?" question and use the criterion of pure emotion to decide if the answer is yes or no. In those instances, we feel happy, excited and alive as we relate to each other, and assume that we must be in love and that he or she is the one for me. This compass uses "feeling" as its reference point for true north and  is not unlike deciding to purchase a car because I feel happy, excited and alive when I get behind the wheel. If that is our criteria, then we'd better be partial to fruit because a lemon likely awaits us when the engine goes sour a short distance down the road, and unforeseen headaches, repairs and expenses greet us.

Is emotion your compass point for deciding if you are "in love"? If so, the misconception that love is just a feeling is leading you down the risky path of setting time, emotional and physical boundaries that are oriented simply toward preserving that feeling and potentially remaining stuck in infatuation. This route doesn't bring us anywhere near true love — it is like being in the forest on a moonless, cloudy night with a compass whose points all read "in the woods." We're not likely to get very far!

As we move through infatuation — those needy times marked by passion and desire — we will be much better off if the true north on our compass reads "compatibility" instead of "happiness."

Compatibility

We usually view compatibility as a good fit between our interests and background and another's interests and background. We enjoy being with someone who is similar to us since this is a powerful source of validation. Have you ever had one of those "So do I!" conversations as you're getting to know somebody?

"You like the outdoors? So do I."

"You like rhythm and blues? So do I."

"You have divorced parents? So do I."

Translated, these conversations usually read, "You're similar to me? Then I'm okay." This is a great feeling, especially if the gauge on our self-esteem meter has been registering a bit low. Identifying compatible interests or characteristics is universally positive, generates joy and builds when we can do the things we enjoy together. Both of us, for example, loved to take walks on the beach, so when we would take them together it would feel wonderful...and still does, twenty-four years later!

Having common interests or similar backgrounds, however, is not enough to orient us toward true love. Real compatibility includes shared beliefs in the big-ticket areas of life such as core values, a sense of responsibility, family, community, spirituality, success and communication. In new relationships, compatible values often translate into compatible time, emotional and physical/sexual boundaries that help to develop a mutual compass for living out a relationship. Like most things, compatibility takes time to identify.

How many times have you or someone you know experienced a relationship that began with both people believing they were compatible, only to find out later that they weren't so similar (or vice versa)? Many people don't show their authentic selves early in relationships when they are trying so hard to get along. This obviously makes it difficult to determine if the face we see is the real person or just good manners. People can portray themselves or act in any way they want, depending on the agenda that drives them, which often makes it easy to think that we see compatibility when it actually doesn't exist. We have a long list of names for people like that (player, shark, siren and the like), but regardless of what we call it, true compatibility is something we come to know only over time. So don't let yourself get in too deep too quickly. It is not that everyone has a conscious, evil intent to deceive, but all of us need time to let down our guard and become comfortable enough to allow our real personalities to come forward.

The initial compass point that we want, then, is compatibility, not simply emotion. This doesn't automatically mean that differences in values or relationship guidelines doom the relationship, but it may mean more of an uphill road, especially if the other person does not respect our values and guidelines, in both words and actions. Remember: actions speak louder than words. If someone claims to value honesty but then you catch that person in a lie, it means that she or he doesn't really value honesty. Integrated values motivate behavior, so if a person claims to share your values but you don't see him or her live them out, a red flag should go up immediately.

Into Intimacy

Assuming our compatibility compass is functional, as the weeks and months of our relationship go by, we naturally begin to feel a deepening desire for intimacy. Have we, however, really considered the meaning of the word *intimacy*? How have you used the word in your relationships?

Just like *love*, intimacy is used in many ways to describe many things: an intimate setting, an intimate knowledge of something, intimate apparel, emotional intimacy, sexual intimacy and so on. We typically associate intimacy with closeness, and so when we say we are intimate with someone, we mean we are "close" to them in some special way. Let's look more deeply at that word *close.*

Thinking about it, the word *close* is often associated with positive experiences, but it can also imply an incompleteness. Almost made that putt...it was close. Try that math problem again...your answer was close. Nice toss...close to a ringer. Closeness in relationships sounds like a great thing and no doubt it feels awfully good. Closeness should not, however, be mistaken for intimacy.

True intimacy is oneness. It is union of our soul with the soul of another. Intimacy is the complete union of one person with another person and it is based on total truthfulness and honesty. Anything short of this soul-sharing unity may be "close," but it is not intimacy because it is incomplete.

In pursuing our desires and infatuations, we always experience some level of closeness. Sharing time together, sitting together, talking together, laughing together, working together, doing things for each other all produce a sense of closeness. The cards, letters, e-mails and thoughtful gestures we exchange produce close feelings that are natural, but this is not yet intimacy. Having set good boundaries, these experiences act as important seeds for growth, but to successfully meet the challenges of lasting relationships, we need a set of skills to keep us moving in the right direction: communication skills.

Communication

The precursor to true intimacy is communication — the open and respectful, verbal and nonverbal give-and-take that marks healthy relationships. How do you rate yourself as a communicator?

As our own relationship moved toward "closer," we

struggled with communication. Donna came from a family that often engaged in personal communication. She had been a facilitator in retreat programs since high school, which helped her learn to express her thoughts, feelings, hopes, fears and dreams both verbally and through poetry. Tom, on the other hand, came from a family background of divorce with minimal personal sharing among family members and limited social experiences in which emotional communication was required. Given these backgrounds, initial conversations usually had Donna talking and Tom listening, since he worried that

Donna might think his thoughts and feelings were stupid. Over the years, we reached a better balance but that took work, risk and working through the disillusionments caused by lack of open communication.

Open communication allows the early forerunners of emotional intimacy to develop, since words are a primary medium through which we come to know the truth about how each other thinks and feels. It is one tool for identifying compatibility. Our likes, dislikes, joys, hurts, values, expectations, assumptions, desires, past experiences and core wounds all have to be spoken if they are to be fully known to one another. Sharing this fabric of our personhood provides us with the feedback that we are accepted for who we are despite our woundedness.

In your relationships, how would you describe your style of communicating? How did you decide how much to share, when to share it and with whom to share it? Our reference point of "graduality" applies again, since putting too much of ourselves out too quickly may lead us to feel close, but conversely can create more confusion in a relationship than clarity. Our best bet is not letting it all hang out too early, which creates strong, sometimes confusing, emotional bonds before the relationship is ready for it, or before we're confident in trusting the other person to respect us and our feelings. Also, quick emotional bonds of closeness often lead to sexual closeness that creates further closeness-intimacy problems.

Physical Closeness

As time progresses and we spend more and more time together, our feelings of closeness naturally pull us physically closer to one another. We want to touch each other, hug, cuddle, hold hands and kiss as we communicate care for one another through the warmth of our touch. This is good — God gave us the ability to relate to each other in this way.

What have these physical gestures of affection meant to you in your relationships? How soon into a relationship do you hold hands, cuddle or hug? If your reference points tell you that you should be physical from day one or, at least, fairly soon, you might want to consider how powerful these physical connections are in creating emotional bonds. The physiological rush and the psychological affirmation from physical closeness can put us quickly into that "I-think-I'm-in-love" mode without a strong communication base, thereby overloading our judgment and weakening our boundaries. Even simple gestures of holding hands or hugging need to be valued and appreciated as treasures in our relationships and not taken for granted.

How far into a relationship should physical closeness begin? As always, it is hard to put a number on it, but for starters, give it a couple of months. "Are you kidding! Don't even hold hands for a couple of months?" the reader asks. "No," the authors answer. "We're not kidding."

Give yourself time to get to know someone first as a friend and foster the basis of trust that he or she respects you before you start to connect physically. Again, we do not want to imply any evil or wrong in this beautiful way of connecting, but the reality is that the power of early physical connections can sometimes put too much pressure on a relationship, weakening its foundation and ability to withstand the challenges of growth it must face in order to endure.

You can often set yourself up for hurt and relationship disappointment with a big kiss on the first date — often because he wants to show her he likes her and she doesn't want to look like she doesn't like him. A fellow retreatant once said that a first-date kiss was an indication that the guy was interested in her. We asked her how she knew that he wasn't a guy who just liked kissing women. Two weeks later, having been "dumped," our friend quipped, "I guess he did just like to kiss women."

Friendship or Sex?

Our relationship compass now has two reference points that help us know if we're heading in the direction of true, lasting love: compatibility and communication. If we can stay on course as our desire for physical and emotional closeness deepens, we begin to experience *philia* — friendship love — the next step in God's design for love. This dimension of love is difficult, if not impossible, to reach and maintain if we act on our desires for wholeness and closeness by beginning to have sex. The world refers to this level of physical closeness as sexual intimacy, but it isn't. Beginning to have sexual relations completely changes a relationship, whether we acknowledge it or not. Regardless of whether it is mutual masturbation, oral sex, anal sex, intercourse or what any other 'is' is, the crossing of the line from external, nongenital closeness to genital contact or internal penetration (including French kissing) can so disrupt the natural course of God's design for love that many relationships that cross it before marriage usually end. The thoughts, feelings and desires for physical closeness are totally normal, but the key, once more, is what we do with them. The best testimony to this we ever heard was from a teenage girl who said, "I've had sex with guys before and if there's one thing I've learned the hard way, it's that sex can ruin a great friendship."

This is not in any way to say that, sex is a bad thing. God created sex, so not only is it not bad, but sex is a good, beautiful gift from God, as are the sexual feelings that we experience. Sexual relations should be tender, loving expressions of true intimacy designed for friends who are husband and wife, but not designed for friends and acquaintances who are...well, friends and acquaintances.

The young woman's statement that sex hurts a friendship is accurate because a relationship that is sexual without marriage can — even without intending it — put pleasure on a higher pedestal than person, thereby undermining the respect and honor necessary for true love. Many people argue that this is not true, noting that they were sexually active before marriage, did respect and honor each other and continue to do so now in their marriage. In these situations, it is more likely a testimony to that couple's resilience and ability to grow toward emotional and spiritual wholeness within their marriage than it is evidence that the principle is wrong. We obviously cannot judge any individual case. Our experience, however — be it personal, clinical or otherwise — does support the facts and reality described earlier that reserving sex for marriage results in a fuller experience of intimacy for a couple down the road, and helps to prevent difficulties on physical, emotional and spiritual levels (more on this in a bit).

Intimacy, remember, is soul-sharing oneness, the complete union of one person with another: mind, spirit and body. Sex outside the commitment of marriage is physically close, is usually emotionally close, but isn't "intimate." Two people's bodies may be physically united, but the complete union that marks true love requires the mind and spirit to be honestly a part of that union as well. We are often amazed by the many couples on TV and in real life who can be so mistrustful and despise each other in so many ways, yet talk about how great their "sexual intimacy" is, as if it were something separate from their relationship. "Yes, I know she cheated on me, but our sexual intimacy is still terrific." True sexual intimacy can only be present when an unconditional, permanent love has been committed to inwardly and has been outwardly proclaimed, lived out day after day and been proven over time. In its absence, being physically close is not intimate, because the fullness of our souls and the completeness of our being is not a part of our sexual closeness and places us at risk for taking each other for granted, thereby seeing the other as an object for self-gratification, not as a person. In these cases, sexual acts are not acts of love or acts of intimacy. They are acts of closeness and emotion...close, but not complete.

What do we do, then, with our sexual desires as our feelings of love deepen? What do we need to do to keep the necessary boundaries around our communication and compatibility so that our relationship can continue to move toward a lasting and true love? We need the virtue of chastity.

Chapter 10
Chastity

A New Perspective

Have you ever wondered about the reaction Galileo evoked from scientists and theologians back in the early 1600s when he started to insist that the earth wasn't the center of the solar system? This wasn't a new idea — Copernicus had talked about it a century earlier — but it did contradict a centuries-old conventional wisdom that the sun revolved around the earth. Can't you just hear the talk...:

"Can you guys believe him?"

"What an idiot! He must be drinking."

"How totally unrealistic!"

"He is so out of touch with reality."

"The sun the center of the solar system? C'mon."

Now fast forward to the reactions some of us receive when promoting chastity in light of decades of "conventional wisdom" born of the sexual revolution. While the concept of chastity is certainly not a new perspective, sometimes it sure seems like it is. We know now that Galileo was right and scientists and theologians eventually came around,

but things often take a bit longer in matters of morality compared to astronomy, especially when the "proofs" are based more on experience and less on hard science.

"The world is passing through troubled times. The young people of today think of nothing but themselves.... They are impatient of all restraint.... As for the girls, they are immodest and unwomanly in speech and dress."[3]

Can you guess who said that? William Bennett? Pope John Paul II? The U.S. Catholic bishops? Nope. It was Peter the Hermit in A.D. 1274. If old Peter checked out the downtown mall this week, we think he'd add a line for the boys too! Our point is that while speaking about sexual restraint and waiting for sex until marriage is not a new concept, it is still not well received in many circles. Even though there are signs that this mind-set may be slowly changing, discussion of chastity is usually still met with a good deal of skepticism.

In the previous chapters, we've been identifying reference points for relationships that can guide us to true love.

Are most people open to the wisdom of compatibility? Yes. Are they open to the wisdom of communication? Yes. Are they open to the wisdom of chastity? Well.... Our hope is that, if you are a chastity skeptic, you will still read on with an open mind. Even Galileo had a chance to present his case! Chastity is more than a mere theory, however; it is a necessity for reaching true, lasting love, and is important to love's journey whether we are single or married.

One Word Is Worth a Thousand Pictures

My (Tom's) first introduction to the word *chastity* was watching a 1970s Woody Allen movie segment about a chastity belt on a medieval woman — the belt being a locked, metal-plated, oversized g-string with the only key held by her husband. Needless to say, chastity was portrayed here as restrictive and negative — an archaic boundary to fun, free love and adultery.

What is your understanding of chastity? What image does the word bring to mind? For many, the concept of chastity evokes negative pictures, sometimes with a crusty priest or nun hovering in the background. In reality, however, this is not a clear picture. Chastity is something positive. It is a marvelous gift, and while it's true that chastity does mean not having sex until you're married, to leave it at that severely limits its meaning. Chastity is God's gift of power, delivered to us by the Holy Spirit, which gives you and me the ability to nurture love and protect our hearts and the hearts of others by helping us choose friendship over sex. Remember, we're poised for the transition from love as desire to love as friendship and goodwill, and the power of chastity brings us there.

Think of chastity as an intangible energy. As we write this, we've been watching the summer Olympics and have witnessed many incredible gold medal performances by athletes who were never expected to win. How did they do it? They were fueled by the intangible energies provided by their dreams, desires, attitudes and discipline, and their actions witness to the commitment they give to their sport. Chastity is similar to those intangibles. Chastity is a virtue that values love and guides our sexual instincts toward the service of love, integrating our sexual urge into the development of ourselves as persons.[4] In a sense, chastity helps us become intimate with ourselves, finding a oneness in our bodily and spiritual being, thereby permitting us to become truly intimate with another.[5]

Virtual Effort

Let's examine this further. First, chastity is a virtue, a stable attitude and habit, which God has laced into our sexual urge and which allows us to set healthy boundaries around our sexual desires. It exists, but we have to activate and perfect it through a combination of prayer, education, effort and freely chosen self-control. This self-control is a fruit of the Holy Spirit within us, as is chastity, and has been present within since our creation. In other words, just like those Olympic athletes, we've got what it takes within us already, but we need to work to develop it to its fullest potential.

Loving Service

Next, chastity guides our instincts toward the service of love, namely, true love. We hear in that phrase "the service of love" an echo of our discussion about love as goodwill and friendship. Goodwill is the desire to live for another in ways that help that individual become the person whom God created him or her to be without demanding anything in return. Chastity is the energy that allows us to place our desire to see our friend grow to his or her fullest potential as a person above our own self-centered desires. It's the part of our guidebook that helps us to put *person* before *pleasure*, to *be* for the other and not use that person for our own physical, psychological or social gain. Living this way, we will naturally set boundaries on our emotional and physical closeness and choose not to become sexually involved. As a result, our friend feels affirmed in worth, value and dignity as he or she sees we are interested in the whole person, not in an experience that is only skin-deep. Chastity, then, validates our friend's identity and self-esteem and serves as a type of salve that can help heal core wounds from childhood or wounds from past relationships. All in all, chastity is a profound service to those we love.

The Road to Oneness

What about those next lines? Chastity...integrates our sexual urge into the development of ourselves as persons...finding a oneness in our bodily and spiritual being. Essentially, this is an example of Jesus' teaching that whoever gives up his or her life will find it. In chastity, as we set boundaries, exercise self-control, embrace our passions with understanding and respectfully hold off on sexual activity, we're not withdrawing into relationship limbo. Instead, chastity is an active, engaging process in which we live out compatibility and communication, deepening our knowledge of ourselves and of our friend.

In our own relationship, we chose to save sexual intercourse until we married, and over the four and a half years of dating and engagement, we learned much about ourselves emotionally because we were challenged to deepen our love for each other in emotional and spiritual ways. We didn't have much of a clue as to what chastity's deeper meaning was back then, but we can testify to the growth we both experienced by practicing it.

Self-Mastery

Self-growth comes not only from learning about ourselves emotionally and spiritually, but also through the exercise of self-control. The choice to not express sexual desire through sexual action leads to the development of self-mastery, the confidence that we can choose to do the right thing even when our hormones urge us otherwise. This translates into self-validation or the affirmation of our own worth, value and dignity, which allows us to be less dependent on others for the validation of our feelings, importance and worth. So, in the end, chastity helps us to bring together the physical, emotional and spiritual sides of ourselves into a unity of body, mind and spirit.

Freedom

Ultimately, living chastity means freedom — freedom to love as God has called us to love. Unlike the common secular definition, freedom does not mean the license to just do what feels good. Freedom is the opportunity to choose to do the right things...the things that *God* wants us to do. On the journey of relationships, God hopes for us to love purely and respectfully, just as he loves. Chastity is also freedom to grow and freedom from selfishness.

In conclusion, then, "chastity is not to be understood as a repressive attitude. On the contrary, chastity should be understood rather as a purity and temporary stewardship of a precious and rich gift of love, in view of the self-giving realized in each person's specific vocation."[6] As Pope John Paul II puts it, "Chastity by no means signifies rejection of human sexuality or lack of esteem for it: rather, it signifies spiritual energy capable of defending love from the perils of selfishness and aggressiveness, and able to advance it toward its full realization."[7]

What does this mean for you on your journey of love? It means that without chastity, you stay bogged down in infatuation and desire in your struggle to reach genuine friendship. Sure, you'll call your honey your friend, but it will be an incomplete friendship. See, living chastity puts "other" before "self" and helps transform infatuation and desire into true friendship. In essence, you're not saying no to sex, you're saying yes to true friendship. When you choose chastity, you say to this best of friends that you are committing yourself to his or her well-being and will never treat him or her as anything other than a person on his or her own journey toward love of self, others and God. That commitment of goodwill allows for the intimacy of friendship — an emotional and spiritual oneness —to become a reality.

This level of intimacy is in many ways the greatest intimacy of all, even after marriage. The absence of mind and spirit in married love makes sexual intercourse just a physical act. Sexual intimacy, even in marriage, needs the oneness of body, mind and spirit, otherwise it is nothing more than just sex.

Chastity Or?

So this is the positive picture of chastity and its positive outcome. Chastity and the growth in integrity we experience through prayer, effort, free-will choices, self-discipline and self-mastery provide us with what we need to successfully journey toward our destination of true, lasting love.

What happens if we don't choose chastity and have sexual relations outside marriage? Where will this lead us?

Chapter 11
Sex Effects

Choice Influences

Has your experience of relationships included any sexual activity prior to marriage? (We're referring to sexual relationships or situations entered into by choice, not sexual situations that are forced upon us, like rape or sexual abuse.) If you have had nonmarital sex, why did it happen? What reference points, influences or rules of love led you to make that choice? People get sexually involved for many reasons, both planned and unplanned, so let's look at some of the major external and internal influences on our decisions and actions.

External Influences

Sex as the norm. Given the sexual shaping of society over the past half-century, it becomes easy to believe that sex in a dating relationship is natural, normal and expected. Natural, we're told, because it's the way we find love, show affection and express our sexuality; normal because everyone is doing it. If you're not sexually active, society reasons, you're somehow abnormal, and who wants to be that? We

referred earlier to family, peer and media influences on our
views of love through the images they portray. Images of
sexual activity between unmarried people far outnumber
those of married sex. The profusion of "love = sex = normal"
messages in all forms of media places pictures of sex for
pleasure deep into our guidance systems and makes it easier
to say to ourselves, "Sex? Well, yeah...okay."

Sexual pressure. Pressure from our peers or pressure to
have sex from someone we're involved with often directs
our choice for sexual activity. Our boyfriend or girlfriend
wants sex and we give in for whatever reason (maybe fear
of rejection), or friends egg us on. We know a young man —
a virgin — who during his first month of college was told
by dozens of guys in the dorm that he was crazy for not
having sex, since there were so many girls on campus "ripe
for the picking." Any way you cut it, this is a very uncomfortable pressure.

Internal Influences

Curiosity. We've heard about sex, read about it or watched steamy film scenes, so we want to experience it for ourselves.

Pleasure seeking. We want to feel good, so we go for it. Sexual release, the pleasure of physical closeness, sexual stimulation and orgasm can be intense and we can let our instincts take us there — all the way from one-nighters to long-term sexually active relationships.

Seeking emotional nurturance and closeness. At times, because we crave closeness, warmth, affection and the like, sexual involvement becomes the medium through which we can temporarily experience these emotional connections. The misconception that sex equals love is usually at work here.

Seeking affirmation. Not many experiences can tell us we're wanted, special, significant, valuable and worthwhile more intensely than sexual closeness. If we need this kind of affirmation, someone's willingness to go to bed with us is a powerful statement that we're important and mean something. We can seek that message through sex.

Seeking power and control. If we have a sense of ourselves as weak, insecure or vulnerable, we may experience in sexual activity a sense of power, strength and control, especially if we see ourselves as able to please the other person. Having sex lets us temporarily recharge those power cells.

Seeking security and connection. Sex often becomes a way for us to feel connected to another person, and it relieves our fears of aloneness. Being alone can become a major source of anxiety, especially if we're moving into our late twenties and are still single. This worry can lead us into sexual relationships with the hope to escape those fears and find permanence. However, this usually doesn't work.

Testing interest and commitment. Some people don't think they can trust another's love for them until they've had sex. We've heard a girl say, "I never know if it's me he wants or if he just wants to have sex with me, so I should go to bed with him, get it over with and then I'll see if he sticks around. If he does, then I know that I'm loved for who I am." Unfortunately, this usually doesn't work either.

Mistakes. "I didn't really mean to have sex...it just happened." Although this outcome is seldom the result of conscious choice, we often do choose to involve ourselves in tempting situations. Once the sexual "mistake" happens, the belief that, "Oh, well, we did it once so why not keep doing it?" is often not far behind. Perhaps the most frequent reason sexual mistakes occur is mixing alcohol or drugs with relationship situations. These lower our inhibitions and make it harder to set and keep boundaries.

It is rare that any of these influences operates alone in leading us to choose sex, since we are very multifaceted people. Whatever the reason, we're still left with the question, "Why not have sex outside of marriage? Is it so bad?"

Nonmarital Sex and Problems on a Personal Level

Sexually Transmitted Diseases. The first set of problems on a personal level is related to our bodies. The physical risks of sexually transmitted diseases (STDs) are at your doorstep once you've entered into a sexual relationship. The ex-surgeon general, C. Everett Koop, once said that when we have sex with someone, it's like having sex with every one of that person's previous sex partners for the past ten years.[8]

Up until about 1970, there were only two important STDs, syphilis and gonorrhea. Today, the list of significant STDs numbers over twenty-five, and it is estimated that 20 percent of all Americans are now STD positive. This means that one in five of us is infected, and that is just for viral STDs. It doesn't count bacterial STDs such as chlamydia, syphilis and gonorrhea. Over six out of ten infections are in persons under twenty-five, and 80 percent of those infected experience no significant symptoms.[9] Worse yet, in spite of all the "safe sex" hype since the 1980s, condoms as a prevention for STDs, including HIV and AIDS, are a crap shoot at best and even worse at preventing human papillomavirus.[10] The concern becomes astronomical when condom failure rates are compounded over a five– to ten–year period.[11]

Some results of STDs, including HIV infection, are:

- pelvic inflammatory disease
- infertility
- ectopic pregnancy
- cancer of the cervix, vulva, vagina and penis
- AIDS and AIDS-related complex
- death

The use of contraceptives and their side effects can also produce some of these physical concerns as well as other psychological and spiritual difficulties. (Although these issues are beyond our present discussion, we recommend you pursue them in our book, *Intimate Bedfellows: Love, Sex and the Catholic Church* — see the appendix.)

Pregnancy. We have difficulty referring to the creation of a human being as a problem, so we want it to be clear that the child created through intercourse in any relationship is not the problem. The issue is what happens after the pregnancy occurs. And more often than not, this ends up being placed entirely on the woman's shoulders. What issues?

- The physical demands of pregnancy.

- The decision to keep the baby, place the child for adoption or have an abortion, and the consequences of each decision.

Abortion. Foremost, a human being is killed. How our society can still debate the humanness of this child is beyond us, given the level of medical and biological support that now exists. In any event, the physical risks of the procedure for the mother (including infection and infertility), the emotional pain from the abortion itself and the aftermath of post-abortion syndrome for both the mother and father impact for a lifetime.

Adoption. Placing the baby for adoption and saying goodbye to the child created, even though it is usually a better decision than single parenting or quick marriage, is never an easy thing to do. It is so difficult that many women who experience an unwanted pregnancy don't consider adoption as a viable option, saying they could never part with the child they've conceived.

Single parenting. All of the physical, emotional and social demands of parenting are hard enough when both

mother and father are together, but they more than double when one is alone. Single parents lose much of their freedom to spend their time as they wish or to pursue educational or career goals. Increased financial and emotional demands are also never easy.

Rushing into marriage. This option puts one at risk for marrying the wrong person, sets up marital struggles and difficulties down the road and very often results in divorce.

Emotional fallout. We've already looked at many of the emotional consequences of nonmarital sex, which can include low self-esteem, dependency, rejection, abandonment, guilt, fear, anxiety, anger, diminished communication skills, diminished self-respect and confusing sex for love. Perhaps the most damaging effects occur when broken sexual relationships confirm and compound our core fears, leading us to become even more convinced that we are inadequate, unlovable, worthless, not good enough, unimportant and so on.

Problems on a Social Level

The next set of issues to consider are the ways that sex outside marriage can actually damage and limit relationships. There is growing evidence of a connection between sex before marriage and dissatisfaction with eventual marriage and sex life.[12] On the other hand, couples who were sexually abstinent before marriage and believed in premarital chastity have a higher marital and sexual satisfaction in their marriages.[13] This translates beyond just levels of satisfaction in a marriage, as people who are sexually active before the wedding have a much higher divorce rate than those who wait for sex until after the wedding.[14] Because this type of research is correlational, we never get a good explanation of why this happens, but, borrowing from Peter the Hermit, it seems to us that sex before marriage makes it easier to become focused on ourselves and our physical needs, and limits our ability to develop the communication skills that are a necessary building block for true intimacy. In other words, sex and the reference points that lead us into sexual activity make it too easy to take our friend for granted, and to see that person as a source of our own pleasure and satisfaction. We are not challenged to see her or him as a complex person to whom we may commit our lives.

Cohabitation

While sex before marriage is problematic enough to our relationships, we add fuel to the fire if we choose to live together as nonmarrieds. In the 1950s, one out of ten couples lived together before marriage, but in the 1990s, it was about one in three.[15] (We're defining cohabitation as couples who live together before marriage and are sexually active. This does not include men and women who live in the same home, choose not to have sex and stand by that decision.) The "official" theory behind living together has been that doing so sharpens a couple's relationship skills and works out the kinks before they walk down the aisle. If a couple can't work it out, they can split up without going through a divorce, thereby doing a service to society by keeping the divorce rate low. The theory goes on that the man and woman also do each other a service by helping weed out bad marriage material and allowing them to move on to find that true, lasting love.

What sounds good in theory, however, is not proving true in practice. Studies have shown that cohabiting couples are less committed in their relationships[16] and get married less often than couples who live apart.[17] Cohabiting couples are also more likely to cheat on their spouses if they do get married,[18] and they are more likely to think that cheating on their spouses is no big deal.[19] No surprise, then, that couples who live together and then marry have about a 50 percent higher divorce rate than couples who waited to live together until after the wedding.[20] Their poorer communication skills and more frequent conflicts — compared to married couples who never cohabited — contribute to relationship problems for couples who cohabit.[21] Interestingly, the longer cohabiting couples live together before marriage, the more likely it is that they'll eventually divorce.[22]

It seems that what matters most to the men and women who do live together before marriage is the immediate satisfaction of their relationships, not the desire to commit themselves to another for life. If all of this isn't enough, cohabitation brings with it a greater risk of physical abuse by live-in boyfriends and a greater incidence of initiating cocaine use or smoking.[23]

The Role of Pornography

One more threat to lasting love is pornography. It is predominantly used for sexual arousal or self-stimulation as in masturbation, but it can also engender negative attitudes toward women primarily, and dissatisfaction in one's sexual relationship. In virtually all pornography, but especially hard-core porn, persons are portrayed as objects to be used and dominated, leading to intense passion and sexual pleasure. The images generated in our minds create models for sexual experience that usually can't be achieved in real life. When our expectation is that real-life sex should be like the video, film, website or magazine, we become dissatisfied within our sexual relationship and eventually begin to look elsewhere for sexual fulfillment. Place pornography in the equation with sex outside marriage and cohabitation, and you're definitely heading down the wrong road.

Sex and Your Spirit

So, are we saying that nonmarital sex is the source of problems? That's just what we're saying; it creates problems along the road to true love in both personal and social ways. A person may not even recognize this as it is happening, since many of the effects we just discussed might not show up as concerns for a number of years. This is particularly true for spiritual problems that accompany sex outside marriage. It causes problems in one's relationship with God, and alters one's ability to connect with a person on a spiritual level.

Chapter 12
Sex and Spirituality

Sign Language

All of the personal and social problems arising from nonmarital sex are symptoms of what happens when we alter God's design for love to fit into our own self-centered desires. It's like trying to cross a lake on a mountain bike. As much as we want to get to the other side, the bike just isn't designed for travel on water! In the same way, non-marital relationships are not designed for sex; therefore, entering into a sexually active dating or cohabiting relationship to search for true and lasting love can leave us empty. To understand this better, we need to look at the spiritual dimensions of sex that God has built into us and our relationships.

We're all familiar with signs. Stop signs, yield signs, no smoking signs, hospital signs. All of these signs tell us something. We're also familiar with certain signs that we can make with our hands: peace, hang loose, thumbs up, high five and those other gestures beyond a PG rating. These hand signs are a type of body language. They mean something. They communicate a message.

In the same way, we have certain signs in a relationship that constitute a type of body language: holding hands, hugs, a gentle touch or a kiss. These send messages of care, concern and appreciation for one another. These gestures, hopefully, serve as signs of trust, affirmation, value and respect. When we hug someone we've been going steady with for a while, for example, we are saying to our friend, "I honestly care about you, I'm here for you and I value and respect you. You can trust me." As our friend receives and returns our hug, he or she says to us, "I accept and believe in your care, support, affirmation and respect for me and trust that you treasure me. I too care about you and support, affirm and respect you, trusting that you accept and believe that I honestly mean it."

Let's say that after you and I have hugged in this way, I date someone else behind your back. How would you feel when you found out? Hurt? Angry? Sad? Lied to? Sure you would, and the hug I gave you is no longer the sign that you thought it was. No longer would it say to you that you're loved, valued and respected. Instead, it would have you wondering if you've been naive, inadequate and used. Basically, I lied to you with my body. My hug was supposed to be a sign that a mutual love and respect existed between us, but I didn't really mean it.

God Signs

Hold that thought for a moment while we consider the way that God has always used signs to communicate messages to us. In the Old Testament, for example, God used a rainbow as a sign to Noah and his descendants that God would never again send a flood to wipe out people. The rainbow was a sign of God's promise, a special kind of promise more accurately called a "covenant." A covenant is a commitment that will never be broken. God promised it, his people knew he meant it and they trusted that he would never go back on his word.

In the New Testament, Jesus came to us as a sign of God's love for us. Jesus taught us through his words and actions how to love others and how much God loves us. The greatest sign of God's love for us was Jesus' suffering and death on the cross. Jesus of-fered us his body as the ultimate sign that his love for you and me is complete, unconditional and permanent. Just as with the rainbow for Noah, Jesus' total giving of himself testified to the reality of God's love for us. He testified to God's covenant to love us fully, unconditionally and forever. For Jesus to witness to this love, it had to be there before Jesus established the new covenant in his own blood. He gave this testimony to prove how real and permanent this already existing commitment is. It is a commitment that transcends emotion and circumstance, and signifies a total union with us that is fruitful because it leads to the creation of new life in God.

So, what does this have to do with sex? We are created in the image and likeness of God, and our journey of love is about fulfilling that image and likeness by learning to love as God loves — fully, unconditionally, permanently. God has fixed in our hearts the ability to love in this way. The most powerful, personal, truly intimate sign of our love is offering our body to another person through sexual relations, especially sexual intercourse. God's design for sexual intimacy is that it be a sign of a covenant of true, lasting love and a sign of our total, permanent union with our lover. Sex, then, is meant to be a sign that testifies to a permanent covenant commitment existing between a man and a woman, a covenant of complete, unconditional and undying love.[24] This experience of intimacy is a human expression of God's love.

"For this reason a man shall leave father and mother and be united with his wife, and the two shall become one flesh. So, then, they're no longer two but instead are one flesh" (Mt 19:5–6).

Sex as Testimony

For sexual relations to truly be a sign and reflection of God's love, several realities are essential in the relationship:

1. Sexual relations are to be a sign of an existing covenant. In other words, the permanent commitment has to exist first. Jesus' death testified to the love of God that already existed and reminded us of the commitment God had already made. In the same way, God didn't design intercourse to "make love." He planned it to testify to love — a covenant commitment already alive between a man and a woman in marriage.

2. The covenant to which sexual relations testify is to be one of complete, unconditional and permanent love. When Jesus died, he didn't put any limit on God's commitment to love us. He gave himself totally and unconditionally to everyone and there was nothing temporary about it. Since the covenant of love between two persons must also be complete, unconditional and permanent, sexual relations cannot be a part of a temporary or simply "long-term monogamous" relationship. It must be part of a permanent relationship of total and unconditional love.

3. The covenant to which sexual relations testify is to be public as well as private. God didn't send Jesus to go behind closed doors and quietly whisper in the ears of one person that God loves him or her. Jesus' testimony was public and visible to all who looked upon him. Sexual intimacy is designed for relationships in which the permanent commitment between a man and a woman is visible to others as well as known between one another. We're not talking about having sex in public. Rather, we're talking about the visibly proclaimed marital pledge to live for one another over a lifetime.

4. Sexual relations are to deepen the bond of unity between a man and woman and are to be fruitful. The love communicated through Jesus' gift of himself draws us to a deeper unity with God and allows us to become new creations in Christ (cf. 2 Cor 5:14–17). In the same way, sexual relations, particularly intercourse, must be a sign of deepening unity between a man and a woman, and be open to new life.

The only human relationship in which sexual relations can reflect these realities is marriage. Only in marriage can sex be a sign of a covenant and embrace the image and likeness of God. In marriage two people pledge themselves to a permanent covenant in a very public and personal way, committing themselves to be true to one another in sickness and in health, for richer and poorer, in good times and bad times until they die. In doing so, they become a living sign of God's love in the world.[25]

Actually, in a marriage ceremony, a man and woman pledge several things:

1. That their marriage will be "unitive." They promise each other that they will give of themselves day by day in order to nurture their intimacy as they share their hopes, sorrows and joys. The sexually intimate dimension of their

relationship will be both a sign of this unity and serve to deepen it.

2. That their marriage will be "fruitful." Their pledge to be fruitful means that their relationship and sharing of intercourse will be open to new life, or "procreative." Since each time they have intercourse there is the possibility that a new person will be created, commitment in marriage includes a respect for this potential miracle. The language of their bodies in sexual intercourse says that they are open to the possibility of generating new life.

3. That their relationship will be permanent, that is, their commitment to one another will be unconditional and that it will last forever. In marriage, a man and woman promise to love each other for life without holding anything back. They do not say to each other that they hope things will work out.

In order for these pledges to be realized, this love has to be exclusive. Since we're not God, we can't give our body in love to everyone as a sign of an individual commitment to each person. We're called to offer our body as a sign of love to only one person — our spouse. God intends sexual intercourse to testify to our marriage commitment and to reaffirm the faith, hope and love that we promised to each other in our marriage ceremony.

Homosexuality

While the subject of homosexuality has been treated in great depth by many other authors, we would like to focus on a couple of issues relevant to our discussion of true love. The dynamics of homosexuality have triggered a great deal of controversy over the years and also a great deal of pain, fear, anger, hurt and resentment, and our hearts and prayers are with those who have experienced these struggles.

We hope we have been able to make clear that one of the central principles of love is the worth, value and dignity of every human person. "Every" means all. All human persons, whether they are attracted to members of the opposite sex or the same sex, possess the essence of human value and deserve respect. Our faith teaches this and our actions toward persons professing a homosexual inclination need to reflect this.[26]

The problem, however, is not with same-sex attraction. The problem is that homosexual acts are outside God's design for the development of true love, since they do not have the potential to create new life and do not enrich or deepen the love of spouses in marriage. Homosexual sex, then, is contrary to God's plan for love in the same ways that heterosexual sex outside marriage is outside God's design. The same physical, emotional, social and spiritual difficulties that accompany male-female sex outside marriage accompany homosexual sex.

The principles on which this understanding is based go way back in our history (e.g., see Lev 20:13), but this understanding has been confused by the sexual revolution, the gay rights movement and, more recently, the push for homosexual civil unions, belief in a homosexual person's inability to change his or her lifestyle and research reports of a biological basis for homosexuality. Marriage, however, has always been understood to be a sacred union of one man and one woman and, as we've stated, it is sacramental in that it is a living sign of God's love in the world.

In terms of biology, there is no evidence that homosexuality has a genetic cause. Very few research studies have found a correlation between homosexuality and either organic or genetic factors in homosexual men, and such correlations for women have not been found.[27] Change from a homosexual to a heterosexual lifestyle, while certainly difficult, is possible and has been widely documented.[28]

While the debate will likely continue for some time, our concern is for the persons engaged in a homosexual lifestyle or those struggling with same-sex attractions because their journeys of love are so difficult. If you are experiencing such difficulties, seek out a counselor, a spiritual director or another person who can support you with positive, God-centered knowledge and help you to live a God-centered love. If you are actively living a homosexual lifestyle, our hope is that you can open yourself to the transforming power of God's love for you and find a return to true love's path. Gay or straight, we are all called to live the virtue of chastity and can all find our way to do so if we commit ourselves to it.

Problems on a Spiritual Level

Choosing sex outside marriage is, first and foremost, a challenge to God's plan of love. Even though we may not be conscious of God's natural design of love, our choice for sex begins to place a wedge between God and ourselves. Just like a player who refuses to do what her coach asks of her and hurts the team chemistry, nonmarital sex impacts the spiritual chemistry between us and God, leading us to distance ourselves from him. The more this chemistry is out of balance, the more self-centered we can become, leading us to mistake lust for love.

Lust versus Love

Lust is the "disordered desire for or inordinate enjoyment of sexual pleasure."[29] Lust is pleasure sought for itself and separated from the unitive and procreative qualities of sexual relations. More than simply noticing attractive men or women for a moment and having a sexual thought about them, lust is more obsessive. It leads us to act on our attraction and desire in a way that splits our bodies from our hearts and renders sex void of its ability to reflect true love, friendship and interpersonal unity. As a result, lust moves us farther away from God.

In the process, lust can lead us to challenge God in other ways that, in turn, continue to move us farther from the heart of God. This is why we refer to lust as a "capital sin." Consider how the effects of lust can position us against some of God's commandments.

The 1st Commandment: "You shall not have other gods besides me." Sexual pleasure is so immediately rewarding that it can become in itself an idol of worship. This broad spectrum can run from obsession with pornography to ending a marriage because our spouse is not "sexually satisfying."

The 5th Commandment: "You shall not kill." We're not suggesting here that lust will actually lead someone to physically kill another person, although crimes of "passion" are frequent enough. On a spiritual plane, however, because sex creates such strong psychological bonds, the resulting hurt from a broken sexual relationship can make a person feel as if a part of her or him has died. Saying something like, "the pain is killing me," acknowledges just how deep the wound actually is. After a failed relationship, depression leading to suicide is not unheard of.

The 6th Commandment: "You shall not commit adultery." Lust goads a husband or wife toward extramarital affairs, often disguising itself as the desire for emotional affirmation, validation and the experience of being loved, wanted or special. Just as Satan tempted Jesus with what he thought would fill Jesus' needs, so are we tempted through what we feel we need psychologically or emotionally.

The 8th Commandment: "You shall not bear false witness." Lust always results in false witness. Acting on our sexual desire outside marriage does not testify to a complete, unconditional, permanent and exclusive love. In this case, we are lying with our bodies.

The 9th Commandment: "You shall not covet your neighbor's wife." Lust's other name is coveting. To covet is to long to possess something that is not ours. This can lead us to extramarital affairs, but even when we are single, we can covet the body of a co-worker, that girl or guy in church, and so on.

Lust also opens a door through which we walk farther away from God by making other things in our life more important than he is (e.g., money, work, success, etc.), by not being life-giving or by being unfaithful, dishonest and covetous in dimensions of life other than sexual relationships. Given the culture that most of us have grown up in, we might not have an adequate understanding of how these things are connected, or more specifically, how choosing sex outside marriage hurts our relationship with God. In a way, we end up cheating on God.

False Witness

In addition to hurting our relationship with God, rejecting God's design for love and sexuality hurts our relationship with the person we now love, or someday hope to love. Remember that for love to be lasting and true, it must possess true intimacy — a oneness of mind, body and spirit wrapped by a covenant of total, unconditional and permanent commitment. When love is true, sexual intimacy reaffirms that commitment which can only be present after marriage.

Choosing to have sex outside marriage actually undermines true intimacy because the spiritual dimension of sex isn't fulfilled. Since nonmarital sex does not testify to an already existing public and private pledge of permanent love, when we have sex with our boyfriend, girlfriend or fiancé(e), whether we recognize it or not, we are bearing false witness to each other. Our bodies and emotions may be passionately united, but because we're not fully spiritually united through the sacrament of marriage, our sharing is incomplete. Whereas sex is designed to say that we are fully united, somewhere in the deep wiring of our brains and the recesses of our hearts, we know that our actions and the intended meaning of our actions do not match. Not being true to God, to oneself or to our lover eventually prohibits a relationship from reaching full psychological and spiritual intimacy. Down the road, this will inevitably create difficulties in the relationship, if it doesn't lead to the end of the relationship itself.

"Partners"

The term *partners* seems to have become the most common word for describing two people in a love-sex relationship. Even mattress commercials ensure "you and your partner" a good night's rest! The problem with this term, as we see it, is that partnerships by their nature are not permanent.

Partners can be formed by assignment ("You two will be partners for this task"), choice ("Would you like to be my dance partner?") or by business contract ("Sign here"). Officially speaking, partnerships are formed by contract or agreement, and they are conditional in that the partners agree to work toward a common goal. Partners usually have certain options to dissolve the partnership if one of them wants to. In other words, it is a relationship of "if-thens": if things are working, then we'll choose to continue. If things are not working, well then.... The liability and length of the relationship is open and limited.[30]

In a relationship, having a temporary partner is very different from relating to a permanent spouse. The permanence of true love requires unconditional commitment to the relationship, regardless of circumstances and without any if-thens. True love is covenant love, not simply a contract love. Sex in marriage is the signature of our souls on that covenant, not a signature of emotion and desire on a mere contract. Only marital sex can testify to an unconditional and permanent covenant; sex with a "partner" cannot.

Just Call Me "Bond"

Sex is wired for bond-formation. God did the wiring so that a married couple could deepen the inseparable bond

between them. A sexual bond of physiology, emotion, psyche and spirit is created when two people experience sexual closeness together. It is intended to be formed one time with one person, not over and over with many people. Each time a sexual bond is formed and broken, part of our soul-bonding ability is lost, making it that much harder to reach true intimacy in a future relationship.[31] Like a wax seal on a letter of commitment, sexual intimacy, once broken, is never quite the same again.

In a way it is like trying to use the same bandage over and over again. The first time I take the bandage off, it loses some of its ability to adhere to my skin when reapplied. The second or third time, it bonds even less effectively, and eventually the bandage loses its ability to bond at all.

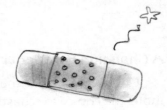

In love relationships, each time we sexually bond with a different partner, we lose some of our ability to form lasting, truly intimate, soul-sharing bonds of oneness. As the number of broken bonds increases, we invariably end up in relationships potentially void of lasting spiritual-emotional bonds.

Moving Toward Chastity

Earlier we identified chastity as the virtue that serves love through freely chosen self-control and which leads us toward our destination of true, lasting love. Now, after having looked at the physical, social and spiritual consequences of not choosing chastity, we hope we have explained why compatibility and communication, without chastity, will not get us to our ultimate destination.

So what do we do if we want to live the virtue of chastity in our relationships? As our compatibilities and communication lead us to stronger feelings of closeness, how do we handle our sexual feelings in healthy ways? And what do we do if we have already been sexually active outside marriage?

Chapter 13
Choosing Chastity

A Changing Perspective

Contrary to what the present cultural norm may promote, the choice for chastity is a very common and positive decision. Virginity until marriage has become more and more popular in our culture,[32] and most married couples remain faithful to one another after the wedding.[33] Married couples, in fact, seem to be much more satisfied with their sex lives than sexually active singles.[34] It is unlikely that many of us would choose something we didn't think was good for us, so it is important to know that the choice to reserve sex for marriage isn't just common — it pays dividends.

The first positive is actually the lack of negatives: chastity allows you to stay clear of all the physical, social and spiritual downers we have just reviewed. Second, chastity gives us:

- the freedom to control our lives and pursue our life's goals without the extra weight of STDs, AIDS, unwanted pregnancy and the like;

- the freedom to develop friendships without the pressure and anxieties of sexual activity;

- the chance to develop our communication skills and abilities in order to be emotionally intimate;
- the opportunity to build our self-esteem through increased self-awareness, self-respect, self-control, self-discipline and self-mastery;
- the opportunity to work toward and experience true love;

Chastity gives others:

- the chance to feel valued and loved for who they are as persons, knowing that they are not objects for our pleasure;
- the chance to build their communication and emotional intimacy skills.

Chastity in Action

Once we accept the positive contributions chastity can make in our lives, there are several ways we can nurture it into a personality style. First, we need to keep chastity a very conscious choice — one that often doesn't come easily, especially as a relationship with a boyfriend or girlfriend grows closer. To help nurture your choice and the relationship, some pro-love guidelines can be set in place.

The most important guideline is to have clear expectations — for yourself first, that you will not cross the sexual boundary line of genital stimulation. Next, if you notice your feelings for each other beginning to grow strong, be proactive and talk about it. Set mutual expectations in advance for your time together. We all know that feelings of affection are hard to keep within boundaries, so prior discussion and mutual commitments that say, "I value you for the person you are and will respect you," can help you stay on the right track.

It is also important to avoid creating situations that will take you farther than you want to go. A colleague recently described an early dating relationship with a girl he felt very attracted to. Several weeks into the relationship after a great night out, she invited him to her house for coffee. He had not intended any type of sexual encounter, but described the struggle of emotion versus reason as they were kissing on the living room couch — in view of her bedroom with the door open and a candle burning on the night table. He let the passion build to that "point of no return," and they ended up in bed. The next day, they both experienced guilt feelings, and a month later, they broke up. His moral for his story? "Played with fire, got burned." What guideline can

help in this kind of situation? Make the choice to leave the cover on the matches. Don't put yourself into situations where affections can ignite into passions that override judgment.

As a corollary to this, avoid mixing alcohol or drugs into a relationship. Things like alcohol, pot, cocaine and related substances are guaranteed to undercut commitments to chastity, so steer clear. The odds are that all of us can tell at least one story of someone we know who made bad sexual

decisions while under the influence, not to mention inci-
dents like date rape, violence or abuse. Plan your time together and leave substances out of the picture.

So, to live out chastity, set clear expectations and guidelines individually and as a couple, avoid sexual set-ups and
say no to drugs and alcohol. Ultimately, it comes down to
choosing a God guideline: if you wouldn't invite the Lord
into the scene of what you're about to do, don't do it.

What If I've Already Had Sex?

Tricia was a young woman in her mid-twenties who had
recently ended a long-term relationship with her boyfriend.
Several months later, she met a great guy and began dating
him. She was experiencing an intense struggle in her new
relationship, however, feeling confused about whether or
not to let the relationship become sexual. She had been sexually involved with her previous boyfriend, and while she enjoyed the physical closeness, she also felt that she had
eventually been taken for granted. During a conversation I
had with her one night, she said, "I guess I might as well go
to bed with him; it's not like I'll be a virgin on my wedding
day anyway."

Tricia's assessment of her situation amounts to something like looking at one's current job and concluding, "Well,
I've always had this kind of job; therefore, I'll never be able
to have a different kind." Tricia was assuming that because
she was no longer a virgin, the gift of her sexuality had been
devalued and would be less meaningful both to her and to
her future husband.

It is critical for us to accept that this is simply not true.
Whereas Tricia — or any of us — may no longer be a physical virgin, we're just a decision away from restoring our psychological, emotional and spiritual virginity through the

choice of chastity. Recall that chastity is that intangible energy — a virtue — that guides us in the service of love and
helps us to grow as persons. God placed this energy in us
as a fruit of the Holy Spirit within, and it doesn't disappear
because we have had sex with someone. It may seem dor-
mant, but we can bring it back to life.

Think of it as being similar to a cell phone battery. Using the phone drains the battery, but once it's drained, we
don't toss it away, saying, "Oh, well, it's no good anymore."
Of course not. We plug it into the energy source and recharge it.

By plugging back into the energy source for our sexuality — God — and recommitting ourselves to live God's design for love, we can recharge our ability to choose purity
and self-control and put ourselves back on the path toward
true love. This choice can actually deepen the meaning and
value of sexual intimacy and put the "-uality" back into sex.

Jesus' forgiveness of the adulterous woman (Jn 8:1–11)
affirms God's healing love for us and points to our "re-
chargeability." There she was, frightened and ashamed,
about to be stoned to death. Jesus challenged the people:
whoever was without sin should throw the first stone. After no one delivered and they had all walked away, Jesus
told her that he did not condemn her. He said, "Go your
way, and from now on sin no more" (Jn 8:11).

If we have been sexually active outside marriage, Jesus
does not condemn us either, but how can we "avoid this
sin"? As difficult as it may seem, we can do so only by choosing chastity. That's what the woman in the Gospel would
have had to do: commit herself to loving as a friend, setting
boundaries, improving her communication and other relationship skills. She would have to develop self-awareness,
self-control, self-acceptance and self-mastery, while learn-

ing to be emotionally intimate without the genital contact. She'd have to express her affection to others without letting herself become aroused to the point of passion-overload, and in so doing, learn the true value of both her own human dignity and that of others. Having reclaimed her chastity, that secondary virgin[35] would have to understand the plan of God, in which only sexual intercourse with her husband could testify to true committed love. Finally, she would have to accept God's will in her life, allowing her to fully know wholeness in the heart of God.

Just as the woman in John 8 was reconciled to Jesus, the sacrament of Reconciliation can help us in this process as a conduit of forgiveness and healing when, through our actions, we have distanced ourselves from God. Through Reconciliation and God's grace, we are also strengthened in the ways needed for chastity to be recharged. So, if you've been sexually active or if you are now, we offer you three words on chastity: *go for it!* Even if you are engaged to be married and have been sexually active with your fiancé(e), the gift of comeback chastity to your future husband or wife will be a blessing to your relationship in ways you cannot imagine.

A Last Word on Chastity

Since the psychological and spiritual dynamics of chastity are complex, it is our hope that you will learn more about chastity and its place in your life from other sources listed in the appendix. For many of us, depending on our education and experience in family and love relationships, we may need some help in choosing or reclaiming chastity. Support from like-minded friends, professional psychologists and counselors, clergy, supportive family members and so on may be necessary for us to reenergize. If this is the case for you, seek out the help you need. It can be uncomfortable to begin such a process, but know that the rewards are great. God will place along your path the people you need to help you move forward on your journey.

Where Are We, Anyway?

This discussion of sex and chastity is pretty thick stuff, so let's get reoriented. We've looked at our relationship experiences and reference points that have guided our relationship decisions in the attraction and desire phases of love. We've tried to describe how compatibility, communication and chastity help us move toward true, lasting love. With these three C's as tools to form deeper, truer friendships, let's examine our experiences of friendship more closely.

Chapter 14
Friendship and Betrothed Love

From "I" to "We"

We have already spoken of chastity as the energy that transforms a relationship from attraction and desire to one of goodwill and friendship by focusing on the well-being of the other. Compatibility, communication and chastity infuse our relationship with mutual affection, concern and compassion that form a true bond of friendship. This is the movement from "I" to "we." In your experience, at what point did you begin to consider a boyfriend or girlfriend a true friend? How have you defined friendship in the context of a love relationship?

Looking back, Donna and I can see that a true bond of friendship formed about six or seven months into our relationship. After becoming "interested" in each other, Donna graduated from college, and we got together several times over the summer. We kept in touch through phone calls and long letters. The following fall, we managed to see each other for great weekends of fun and closeness, sharing our joys and struggles of the weeks in between. The special things

we did for each other, like sending cards or making surprise visits, not only boosted our morale but also began to
instill in us a growing sense of "we."

As you look back, hopefully your stories of friendship
share the same understanding of each other's doubts and
fears, thoughts and dreams. The fun, closeness, caring, support, laughter, respect and peace of friendship nurture us
toward feeling the wholeness we all seek. This nurturance
grows out of a mutual commitment to love with the well-
being of our friend as our priority. True friendship, however, is not measured only by the heights of our joy. It is
also measured by a growing resilience of the bond between
us during times of struggle and disillusionment.

Eighteen months into our relationship, Donna and I were
living in different states. After a wonderful weekend together, we were saying goodbye at the train station when
Donna said, "I need some space. I think we shouldn't see
each other for a while." This was the beginning of a difficult period of mutual disillusionment. We had to work
through both the feelings Donna was having at that time
and the fears of rejection I was experiencing.

Seeds or Weeds?

How have you handled relationship disillusionment and
dissatisfaction in the past? What reference points helped you
deal with it? The skills needed to work through relationship rough spots are outlined in 1 Corinthians 13. Living
out these principles at this point in a relationship plants the
seeds of true love, which can later grow into a lasting love.
So when the road gets rough, do you plant seeds or weeds?
Are you...

- patient, or demanding and hostile?

- kind, or mean and sarcastic?
- humble, or arrogant and conceited?
- generous, or selfish and self-centered?
- honest, or dishonest and withdrawn?
- forgiving, or resentful and judgmental?
- faithful, or disloyal and undependable?

Working through disillusionment successfully always requires positive communication and problem-solving skills. Realistically, even if tools such as patience, kindness and forgiveness are present, they alone will not be enough to work through more difficult situations like conflict in relationships rooted in alcohol or drug problems, affairs, abuse and so on. Given either the lack of commitment to change or the nature of addictions themselves, we are not implying that you should make yourself vulnerable to these kinds of things if they are occurring in your relationship.

We are still in the development of friendship, which involves goodwill — the choice to focus on the complete value and good of another. Anyone who does something to use or devalue you in abusive and cruel ways is simply not a friend.

Lovers' Leap: Betrothed Love

If we have learned that we are compatible, that we can communicate, that we can live in chastity and work through disillusionment, then, if we choose to, we are ready to move toward the final phase of the journey toward true love — betrothed love, the full and total giving of ourselves to our friend. It is the unconditional sharing of one's soul with another for a lifetime, nurtured through a freely chosen self-surrender and a commitment to be life-giving. So, how do I know if I'm ready for betrothed love? More specifically, how do I know if the person I'm in love with is the one in God's plans for me? In other words, "How do I know this person is the one for me?"

By the time Donna and I saw the outlines of betrothed love in our own relationship, we had been dating for several years. We were experiencing the emotional intimacy of friendship and the fulfillment of our desires for affirmation, significance and acceptance. We were feeling the sexual urge for wholeness and the desire to focus on each other's well-being. More than these, however, at the time we began to seriously consider committing ourselves to the vows of marriage, we had a spiritual awareness that God had brought us together and meant for us to continue on a path of love as a "we." We can't really give you specifics about how this came about, but we knew that it had. We had heard other couples talk about their awareness that God's plan for their lives included each other, but we were somewhat skeptical, or at least we lacked an understanding of what it was all about.

On an intuitive level, being sure that your boyfriend or girlfriend is *the one* for you is a knowledge that you will come to *over time*. There will be visible, concrete evidence that you can only look for in your friend to validate her or his "rightness" for you. What do you look for? Ask yourself:

- Are we generally compatible?
- Do we accept our differences? (not just tolerate them, but truly accept them)
- Do we share similar values regarding God, success, time, money, sex, children, family, alcohol and drugs, individual versus couple interests?
- Do we respect each other in our words and actions?
- Do I feel valued as a person by him or her, not feeling used in any way?
- Are we willing to surrender ourselves to each other?
- Do we communicate effectively during difficult times?
- Do we solve problems and make decisions well as a couple?
- Are we willing to love each other completely and unconditionally?
- Is God calling us to be together forever?

If you can answer yes to questions such as these, then you should have a pretty good picture that he or she is the one. There is no magic formula for knowing this, however, and psychologists' offices are full of married couples complaining that their spouses have changed. This is why it is important to give relationships time to grow, and especially to take the time to learn if you can work through problems with one another. That way, when you do make your vows "for better or for worse," you can be confident that you have the resilience for a lifelong love.

We are well aware that few couples, including ourselves, actually enter into betrothed love with everything they need to make it work. All of us learn the things we need to learn on the job, so to speak, provided we are committed to learning them. We do, however, have to be willing to do whatever it takes to make it work. No relationship is perfect, and in the vocation of marriage we are called to continue to work on deepening our skills for moving our relationship toward lasting and true love. Only in doing so can we realize our image and likeness to God and love the way God loves.

Chapter 15
When Relationships Don't Work Out

Feeling a Grind

Looking back at the various jobs listed on our work resumés, it is likely that at least one was not a pleasant experience. Workplace difficulties of one form or another often lead to dissatisfaction with our job, co-workers or supervisors, and may result in our leaving that position to pursue a "better" one. We often use the expression that it just wasn't a "good fit."

Just as likely we have experienced relationships that have ended due to dissatisfaction. If you've been through such an experience, how did you deal with it? When did you realize that you were not satisfied with the relationship, and after it ended, how did you respond?

If we had to define it, we would say that relationship dissatisfaction is, basically, relationship frustration. It is an awareness that our relationship is not progressing as we had hoped it would. We're not talking about casual relationships of a few dates here and there, nor are we referring to an occasional slip of the tongue or miscommunication that leads to mild disappointment. Relationship dissatisfaction is a disillusioning pattern of behavior in long-term relationships for which either one of us, or both of us, are responsible. This disappointment is experienced as a deeper pain. It can occur any time over the course of a relationship, but when it does, it usually comes through one of two channels: either our relationship is in conflict or, on a more subtle plane, our heart intuitively senses that something is not right between us.

Conflict

Relationship conflict is most often played out in overt clashes or covert withdrawal. Whether we clash, withdraw or alternate between the two is usually a function of our personalities, life experiences and education in dealing with our feelings. Either reaction is fueled by our belief that we are not being treated the way we think we *should* be treated. Common "should" statements might include:

"You should be spending more time with me."

"You should be more affectionate."

"You should listen to me more attentively."

"You should accept my feelings."

"You should choose me over _____ (others, sports, work, money, etc.)."

"Shoulds" such as these can also be called "need statements"[36] that spring from our core fears:

"You need to show me that I am not unimportant."

"You need to show me that I am not inadequate."

"You need to show me that I am not unlovable."

"You need to show me that I am not worthless."

There is nothing wrong or unusual in our desire to be treated in these ways. But when we elevate our desires to demands in the form of needs and shoulds, we head toward angry conflicts. When our needs and shoulds go unmet we become sad, angry or hurt and often express our anger by aggressively voicing our shoulds or expressing our hurt through withdrawal, avoidance, sulking and so on. These kinds of behaviors are often met with return anger or withdrawal, contributing to cycles of tension and conflict, which in turn produce feelings of dissatisfaction. Dating relationships marked by tension and conflict often end abruptly by mutual decision or when one person terminates the relationship.

Intuition

The second way we can identify that a relationship is in trouble is by intuition or instinct in the absence of direct interpersonal conflict. An awareness in our heart of hearts, often beginning as a quiet gnawing, tells us something is not right with the relationship. The roots of these feelings vary, but generally, we begin to question the rightness of the relationship for any of the following reasons:

- We become uncomfortable with the way we have set time and emotional boundaries, possibly resulting in our feeling smothered.
- We become uncomfortable with sexual involvement or the lack of it.
- We feel a growing desire for independence or a sense that we have "outgrown" the relationship.
- We meet someone new with whom we think we may be more compatible.

Whatever the reason, this kind of relationship dissatisfaction often forecasts the end of the relationship due to a sense of drifting apart — going our separate ways.

When you became aware of relationship problems, how did you handle it? If you've never been there, how do you think you would handle such dissatisfaction in a relationship?

Can We Work It Out?

Most of us don't abandon ship at the first sign of stormy seas. Usually, we secure the hatches and try to ride out the storm. When a relationship has begun to experience difficulty of a nonviolent, nonabusive nature, we have three options for action.

1. *Crawl into our bunk and hold on.* Some of us try to avoid conflict and confrontation at all costs and adopt an unassertive style, hoping that the tempest will calm. Such avoidance, however, often costs us our self-respect, not to mention the relationship itself. Given human nature, the current storm may blow over, but more dark clouds will form behind it.

2. *Shout at the ocean to knock it off.* Those of us not afraid of confrontation will often take some action in an attempt to change the course of the storm, that is, we try to change the person we're dating. This option uses shoulds and shouldn'ts to the max, as trying to convince our partner of the error of his or her ways. He or she *should* be more sensitive, attentive, communicative, gentle or polite, and *shouldn't* be so self-centered, distant, judgmental and sarcastic. These kinds of storms just tend to get worse since it is impossible for one person to change another. Trying to change the course of the storm most often ends up with our boat capsizing.

3. *Take the helm and find the best course through the waves.* The third option, and the best, for trying to work through relationship dissatisfaction is to get control of our own thoughts and emotions and try to communicate constructively to solve our relationship difficulties. Getting control of our feelings comes from gaining control of our way of thinking and shifting out of self-defeating shoulds and shouldn'ts. To do this, we first have to develop a realistic sense of our own worth and value as the persons we are, and see our human worth as independent of another person's acceptance or rejection. No matter how we are treated, we are still the same worthwhile person of dignity and value that we have been since our creation in God's image. In reality, therefore, we can't be unimportant, unlovable, not good enough and so on.

Next, we have to accept the reality that we cannot force anyone to be different, but can certainly state how we want to be treated and how we feel when we are not treated with kindness and respect. Consider the difference: "You should be spending time with me, not your friends. Don't you realize how unimportant I feel?" versus "I'd really like to see more of you and I feel disappointed that you've just spent the last two weekends with your friends."

This kind of confident nondefensive and nonaccusatory assertiveness projects a self-respect that invites the other person to deal productively with our concern, but it can't make him or her do so nor can it control his or her reactions. If he or she doesn't join with us in a mutual problem-solving process, then it is time to ask: is this a person with whom I want to continue in relationship?

Physical Violence and Emotional Abuse

Any incident of violence or abuse, verbal or physical, is reason to end a dating relationship immediately. Such behavior indicates that the person you are dating is either psychologically unbalanced or someone who sees you as an object, not a person. There is no reason to continue dating someone who treats you this way. This may sound like a harsh reaction, but it is a healthy one. Some persons stay in abusive relationships because they think they are called to forgive, especially when the abuser shows remorse and treats them well at other times. We may be called by God to be forgiving, but that does not mean that we are asked to overlook behavior that is hurtful and put ourselves in the position of being hurt again. Forgiveness may involve letting go over time of the resentment, shame and emotional pain we feel because someone has been abusive toward us, but it must not involve a codependence that lets someone avoid accountability for his or her abusive actions.

Some persons stay in abusive relationships because they believe they can change the person into a nonabuser, but as we said before, it is impossible for anyone to change another person. It is important to understand that you cannot be the catalyst for that person's change just because you wish it could happen. Without sincere, long-term motivation for change, professional help, spiritual guidance and the like, patterns of abuse only repeat themselves and often escalate.

Is there ever hope that someone who has been abusive will change and a relationship can work out? Maybe, but it requires years of committed effort and establishing a record of respect for others in close relationships. There is no need to put yourself at risk. If, as you look at your relationship experience, you see a pattern of abusive relationships, we strongly recommend that you seek out a professional psychologist or counselor. These professionals can help you identify the reference points that led you toward problem relationships in order to learn new reference points from which you can make healthier relationship choices.

If you are ever abused in any way, immediately set boundaries between you and the person who has hurt you, and never allow yourself to be anywhere that the behavior can be repeated. If necessary, legal boundaries should be set up through the local police, court restraining orders and so on, so that you can be as safe as possible.

Dead Ends

What should we do if it becomes clear that a relationship will not bring us to the lasting, true love that we desire? Do we stay in the relationship anyway, or end it and begin to move on?

Staying in. If we know that a relationship is at a dead end and still choose to stay in it, we do so either out of fear or out of comfort.

The fear of being alone is, perhaps, the most common fear that keeps us in a dead-end relationship. Our core beliefs and life experiences have taught us that to be without a partner is intolerable.

We fear that if we leave this relationship, we may not find another one. So we bite the bullet and stay. Even if, in the most unlikely of circumstances, we did find someone else, he or she could be worse. So we settle for the current guy or girl.

The fear of failure is not only a fear that the relationship has failed; rather it is the fear that I have failed. This is hard to overcome, especially if we have experienced several broken relationships. This fear becomes magnified by more dysfunction as one becomes aware of a bind: "This has been a bad relationship for a while, so if I end it now, that means I could have ended it earlier and not wasted all this time. I may be a failure for staying in it, but if I leave it now after staying in it for so long, then I'd be a stupid failure. I don't want to be a stupid failure so I might as well stay in this one and just be a failure for trying."

Moving on. If these fears are not present or can be worked through, one should be able to see a clearer road ahead for moving on from a troubled relationship. The following reference points can be helpful once the decision to move on is made:

1. Be timely. Once we're aware that attempts to improve the relationship have been fruitless, it is better to end the

relationship immediately rather than wait. The longer the wait, the more difficult the breakup can be.

2. Be honest and direct. Put clear closure on a relationship rather than hope it will just fade away. By respectfully stating why the relationship is over, we can help to tie up any loose ends. While a face-to-face discussion is usually the best way to go, a phone call or letter is a good "plan B" if you suspect that problems would arise through an "in-person" breakup.

3. Be consistent. If you say it's over, act like it's over. It often happens that someone breaks up on Monday and then is on the phone to the "breakee" by Wednesday. This sends a mixed message that makes the breakup harder and possibly increases the level of future conflict.

4. Be firm. Sometimes the "breakee" will try to keep the relationship going. Try not to put yourself in positions you don't want to be in — especially out of guilt. The more resolute you are, the better it will be for him or her in the long run.

5. Stay in tune with your emotions. Ending a relationship triggers many strong feelings of sadness, emptiness and loss. It is common for these feelings to be present even when we acknowledge a sense of relief that the relationship is over. Stay tuned to these feelings, process them within yourself by way of journaling or reflection and, if possible, talk about them with supportive family or friends.

Second Chances

Should we give a second chance to a boyfriend or girlfriend with whom we've become dissatisfied? Again, the answer is, "Maybe," but not without different, definitive boundaries or expectations in place to help us be objective about the likelihood of change. The specifics of the "second chance plan" will vary from person to person, but, in general, should include a clear "if-then" contingency: "If you can change and show me in the following specific ways for (fill in number) months, then I will consider reestablishing the relationship. If you do _____ again, then I will end the relationship for good." If your boyfriend or girlfriend says in response, "You shouldn't put conditions on me. What kind of relationship is that?" then it is time to walk away. This kind of self-centered response indicates that the prospects for change are weak.

What if you or I want the second chance and our boyfriend or girlfriend wants to end the relationship? Our initial reaction in this situation is always one of rejection. Being told by another person that we are no longer loved and wanted is very difficult to hear, and our response can run a continuum of emotion from shock to depression to anger. Our spectrum of behavior can range from withdrawal to rapid-fire attempts to win back the heart of the other with flowers, phone calls, e-mails and so on. Where we actually fall on these feeling-action spectrums is often determined by the messages we hear coming from rejection, especially if they confirm a preexisting negative view of our self-worth. Let's say, for example, that I entered the relationship thinking, "Maybe I'm not good enough to be loved." If I end up dumped, it is very likely that this fear will be intensified, leading me to become depressed, angry or defensive.

Self-Defeating Reactions

Regardless of whether a difficult relationship ends through our own decision, the other person's decision or a mutual decision, several self-defeating reactions can ultimately limit our ability to move forward toward lasting love in the future: panic, depression and rebounds.

Panic and Aloneness

Once we realize that our relationship is ending, strong fear and panic can set in. The person around whom much of our energy was centered is gone, and we can feel like we've lost our gyroscope. Our time, activities and lifestyle become unpredictable and cause an insecurity that can fire up our fight or flight hormones. This drives us toward other relationships or back toward our ex in the hope of reducing our panic and fear.

A significant fear entwined in panic reactions is the fear of being alone. The experience of aloneness can cause heightened anxiety and require us to face ourselves in ways we may not want to. In order to avoid seeing things in ourselves we don't like, we try to avoid being alone, often hiding the fear that we may end up being alone forever.

Depression

Virtually everyone feels some degree of sadness after a relationship ends, but when that sadness reaches deep, sometimes overwhelming levels, we become depressed. This happens when the loss we have experienced has left us feeling so empty that we become hopeless.

In its most serious form, such sadness and hopelessness take on characteristics of clinical depression, which include sleep difficulties, changes in appetite, lack of interest or pleasure in things we used to enjoy, concentration problems, feelings of worthlessness, fatigue and even thoughts of death or suicide.[37] We develop a negative view of ourselves, our circumstances and our future,[38] and often experience a withdrawal from our usual social connections, sometimes turning to alcohol and drugs to ease the pain.

Should you experience depressive symptoms of this kind, consult with a mental health professional. Sometimes short-term guidance can go a long way in getting us back on the right track.

Rebounds

With or without panic and depression, after a broken relationship we might quickly "bounce off" our old relationship. In physics, "rebound" describes how an object, like a ball, changes direction when movement is blocked by something in its path. The ball has no say in the matter — it just can't continue on the path it was on, so it has to change direction.

Human rebound reactions often seem to follow the same principle. The path we may have wanted to travel with our boyfriend or girlfriend is blocked, so we bounce off that relationship and experience pain, panic, depression, anger, aloneness or feelings of insignificance.

Offensive and Defensive Rebounds

Basketball has two types of rebounds, offensive and defensive. Offensive rebounds refer to grabbing the ball after you or a teammate misses a shot. Once you have it, you try to score again. An offensive relationship rebound describes how we quickly jump into a new relationship after the old one has ended. We couldn't get our previous relationship to go where we wanted it to go, so we grab for another and try to score some points with this new one. Unfortunately, most of us who pick up a relationship on the rebound eventually end up in circumstances similar to our previous relationship, because we retain the same blueprint that guided us in the old relationship.

The other type of rebound is the defensive rebound, usually occurring when someone has broken up with us. In this type of relationship rebound, we don't jump into a new relationship, but, instead, try to restart the old one or begin some form of retaliation against the other person. These reactions almost always involve high levels of panic and anger. That anger can either be directly or indirectly expressed toward our former dating partner. In the latter case, we can act out our hurt and pain by being directly insulting, harassing, verbally or physically aggressive or trying to interfere in our ex-lover's new relationships. More indirectly, we can take out our anger by criticizing him or her to our friends or starting rumors.

Whether our rebound is offensive or defensive, our reactions keep us focused more on our ex-lover and our past — and less on ourselves and our future — preventing us from moving on to healthier relationships.

Controlling the Rebounds

To experience a healthy reaction to a broken relationship, we need to develop a positive focus about ourselves, our circumstances and our future. Creating this trio requires that we take time after a breakup to focus on our thoughts and feelings and accept them as real and valid. If we're sad, we should cry. If we're angry, we should express it in positive ways.

Talking to supportive friends, praying, writing our thoughts and feelings in a journal and so on, are excellent tools for helping us process both our emotions and experiences in ways that help us learn from what we've been through. In addition, it is also important to set solid boundaries around starting a new relationship. A good reference point is to hold off on any dating for a couple of months. This doesn't mean that we can't spend time with opposite-sex friends who are fun to be with or who offer us support. It does mean, however, that we shouldn't pursue any romantic interests. We need time to get our head together.

We should also be sure that we're staying active, eating right, getting rest and following through on any other aspects of healthy living that will serve to keep us in balance. Sure, we'll fall off once in a while, but we have to be clear that just because a relationship has ended, we're not a ball rebounding out of control. We have a say in which direction we want to go and have a much better chance of finding a future path to lasting love if we stay focused, deal constructively with our emotions (avoid panic, depression or retaliation) and take time before beginning a new relationship.

Can We Still Be Friends?

"If we can't get our relationship back together, can we at least stay friends?" Probably not, at least not if your relationship was emotionally intimate. There are certainly exceptions to this, but usually couples who have experienced some form of a best friendship/love relationship have a very hard time relating to each other as nondating friends. This is especially true if there was any sexual involvement. Couples who are able to stay friends seem to be those who have a strong sense of themselves as individuals, have a deep respect for each other as persons and can maintain both when each begins new relationships. At some point, if the new relationship becomes serious, the ex-lovers-now-just-friends need to be distanced if the new relationships are going to work.

Chapter 16
Sexual Assault

Traumatic Experiences

Before we close our discussion of relationship experiences, sexual assault needs to be addressed because it has a significant impact on our relationships and the development of relationship reference points. Sexual assault refers to any kind of sexual action directed toward you that is not desired. It is a product of force and can occur through verbal or physical threats, extortion or acts of violence. Sexual assault includes all forms of actual or attempted rape, date rape, molestation and sexual harassment, and can be perpetrated by anyone, although it is usually committed by acquaintances or relatives.[39] Both men and women can be victims of sexual assault, and it is estimated that approximately 25 to 30 percent of women and 15 percent of men experience a sexual assault in their lifetimes.[40]

If you have experienced any type of sexual assault, be it sexual abuse as a child, rape or date rape, our hearts are with you since we know how deeply your soul has been hurt. We hope that you have been able to seek out the help and support necessary to move toward healing, which is an important part of your overall journey toward true love. Wounds of fear, shame, doubt, worthlessness, mistrust and the like create potentially difficult detours that can keep you off true love's path. This kind of hurt can convince us that we should never trust anyone, thereby preventing us from the possibility of having love relationships. It can push us into one bad relationship after another as we seek the acceptance and security we desire, only to find ourselves more alone and isolated.

The purpose of addressing this painful dimension of relationship experience is to encourage you to keep learning how to set healthy boundaries in relationships, especially those that might keep you safe. Sexual assault is a crime committed by criminals against victims, and no one who is a victim of rape or other forms of sexual assault is at fault because it happened. Victims are generally chosen because of their vulnerability or the criminal's opportunity.[41] We would like to offer two guidelines especially for the early months of a relationship that can help reduce the risk of such assault:

1. Never be alone with someone without a previous history of his or her ability to respect you.
2. Take steps to protect the beverages you drink from being drugged.

Safety in Numbers

Not being alone with someone you're just getting to know may seem unrealistic or overly cautious, but it does make sense. Many sexual assaults occur as date rape or party-rape in which a woman is set up. An invitation to be driven to a movie can seem quite innocuous and reasonable, but once in the car, she becomes vulnerable. An invitation to go upstairs to listen to music at a party can also be a prelude to rape. While most invitations may have no ill will behind them, you are still doing the reasonable thing to minimize your risk.

One way to guide your decision about who to be with and where to go is to view the time you spend with someone and how he or she treats you as evidence for determining his or her respect-potential. This evidence can fall into one of two categories:

Column A	Column B
He or she treated me with kindness, gentleness, patience and the like.	*He or she criticized me, insulted me, physically or emotionally hurt me, used drugs or drank too much, pressured me, intimidated me or made me feel inferior.*

Early dating or times together are better spent in groups or in public, using one's own means of transportation. If during these times, we experience column A, then as weeks or months go by, we have a better ability to predict that we'll be safe when the two of us are alone. If, however, we

Its a GOOD iDea to use YOUR own caR FOR FiRst Dates!

experience anything from column B, it would be senseless to predict that we'll be safe if we are alone, never mind continue the relationship. A true reading, remember, takes time. An employer would never give someone a reference for an important position based on a few weeks of watching him or her on the job. The same test of time should apply to your relationships as well.

Bottoms Up, Lids On

An increasing number of sexual assaults involves drugging the victim by slipping chemicals, such as Rohypnol, into her drink.[42] Such a drug impacts coordination, induces sleep, causes significant muscle relaxation and amnesia and intensifies the effects of other drugs or alcohol. These fast-acting drugs dissolve very quickly in liquid. For these reasons we strongly recommend that you:

- Accept open drinks only from someone you know well; never take one from a stranger.
- Drink from cans or bottles with caps that you have removed yourself.
- Take your drink with you wherever you go. Never leave drinks unattended or out of the hand of a trusted friend.

As careful as we can be, however, tragedies occur. If you have been sexually assaulted, get help immediately. Go to a safe place, report the crime to the police and obtain immediate medical attention. Get support right away from family and friends, or from crisis services that can always be accessed through hospital emergency rooms, local police, shelters and so on. Afterward, commit yourself to the journey of healing. Professional counseling, support groups and spiritual healing are a must, so resist any hesitancy to enter such a healing process because of fear or shame. Remember, you are created in God's image and no criminal act can change that. God wants you to experience love and give love, so seek whatever help you need to work through this trauma, however difficult it may be. Sexual assault disrupts the ability of our heart and soul to love as God loves and to receive his love for us. We must do all we can to move toward fulfilling our call to love and not succumb to the fears that might tell us that true love will never be ours.

THE JOURNEY HOME

Chapter 17
The Big Picture of Love's Journey

More than fifteen years ago, we heard a story with a great message. The person who first told it has our thanks, whoever you are. It is a story of a customs official working at an international border checkpoint. One day a woman riding a motorcycle drove up to the gate, carrying a brown paper bag in her hand. The guard checked it and saw that it was full of sand. "That's odd," he thought. "But there is no law against carrying sand over the border." Her identification papers were in order, so he let her go.

A few days later, the woman again arrived at the checkpoint riding a motorcycle and carrying a paper bag. The guard looked in the bag, and once more found it was full of sand. His intuition was screaming that something was wrong, so he checked the sand more closely, rolling it in his fingers, even tasting it, since he suspected it was a disguised illegal substance. He couldn't find anything. The same scenario took place three more times. Finally, in complete frustration, the official made the woman come into his office where he conducted chemical tests on the sand. Still he found nothing. Angrily he told her, "Look, I've been at this job a long time. I know there's something illegal going on here, but I just can't prove it. I'll make you a deal.... You tell me what you're doing and I won't arrest you this time."

"Really?" said the woman, knowing this would be her last trip. "You won't arrest me?"

"You have my word."

"Okay," she said. "You're right. I'm smuggling motorcycles."

How easy it is to focus our attention on a small detail that we think is important, only to miss the bigger, more important picture. Hopefully, the discussion of love in the preceding pages has provided you with a glimpse of the big picture of relationships necessary to reach your destination of a lasting, true love.

A Review

Our big picture of love has a multifaceted foreground. The figures in this foreground are you and I moving toward a destination where we can love as God loves — completely, unconditionally and permanently. Since we are created in his image and likeness, we begin life with the potential for love woven into the fabric of our being, and must embrace a journey of growth in order to fulfill it.

As you have journeyed through the pages of this book, we hope you have taken the time to build your own understanding of your personal journey of love to this point in your life, asking yourself where you have been, where you are now and where you wish to go in your relationships.

We've asked you to consider your identity: who you are as a person of infinite worth and value, as a creation of God. All of us can grow to more fully accept our goodness as persons and learn to challenge, shift and modify any deeply held negative judgments and beliefs about our worth, adequacy, significance and capacity for love. We've also tried to help you focus on your hopes and dreams for true, lasting love and the education in love you've received since childhood. This instruction comes by way of "institutions of learning" such as family, friends, the media and one's church background, and has provided you with the basic principles for your expectations, conceptions and misconceptions for love and relationships.

We've looked at how past and current lessons in love have played out in your experience of relationships and the development of relationship reference points. These guidelines direct the decisions you make concerning the way you seek and express love. In the course of our discussion, we've offered other God-centered guidelines that can help take you through the progression of love from attraction, infatuation and desire, to friendship, goodwill and betrothed, lasting love. These guidelines have centered on what you can do to set healthy relationship boundaries and allow for the living out of companionship, communication and chastity.

True and Lasting Love

Whether it is the first time around for you in a relationship or whether you've been unable to find the path to lasting love and are looking to start again on this journey, it is easy to end up on the wrong trail. Anyone can lose their way if they believe that love is only romance, emotion, sex or security, and they don't fully understand that true love requires action, commitment and decision. A man and woman move toward true love only when their actions reflect a deep honor and respect for each other's worth as persons, reflected in their decisions to be patient, kind, accepting, forgiving and gentle.

True and lasting love is a product of companionship, communication, chastity and the way in which these synergize into the soul-sharing oneness that is true intimacy. These actions draw their power and meaning from our conscious commitment to live for our beloved over the course of a lifetime. Our acts of love tell our beloved about the reality of our permanent, loving presence in his or her life.

When such loving actions are present in our relationships and we say, "I love you," the word *love* is both noun and verb, description and prediction. In other words, "I love you" describes our feelings for our beloved today, but it also commits us to an eternity of selfless, self-sacrificing decision and effort. True love is a faithful love.

The Importance of Guides

Since love is a journey of action and doing, we need knowledgeable guides who can provide the skills and support necessary to keep our steps heading in the right direc-

tion. Which guide we should enlist will depend on what we need at different points of the trek, but one guide we must always have along is God. The more we keep God as an intimate part of our lives, the more likely it will be that our journey toward true love will be a fruitful one. In the same way that time, commitment and communication help our love relationships grow, spending time with God in prayer, meditation, scripture reading and worship will help our relationship with him to grow as well. Unlike a boyfriend or girlfriend, however, God is always available!

Other guides we may wish to utilize include family members or friends, provided they are role models for where we would like to be in relationships. If we wanted to build a house, we would seek advice from people who are knowledgeable about the process. In building relationships, be they friendships or love relationships, we should look for guidance from people who know how to live these in positive ways. Support from a counselor, a spiritual director or another person can also be extremely helpful, especially if we are experiencing psychological, emotional or spiritual struggles that are making relationships difficult for us. If initially you prefer reading rather than talking, many excellent books about love and relationships can serve as sources of positive reference points. Regardless of how we choose to access guidance, we should remember that our history does not have to control our future, and we can make whatever changes necessary to find, create and deepen the love we desire.

Respecting Respect

Unfortunately, there are no love relationship gurus who can provide all the answers. These authors certainly can't. All of us have been on the wrong path of love at some point

and often wind up back on those same paths during the course of our lives. The key is the willingness to learn and grow in love. Each one of us is a work in progress, and even though we may have made decisions in the past that we wish we hadn't made, we are all able to dedicate or rededicate ourselves to God's design for lasting love.

All relationships that move toward true love share one fundamental characteristic: respect. Respect for the worth and dignity of the person we love generates the setting of every healthy boundary, every decision of goodwill, every step toward intimacy and every commitment to love fully, unconditionally and forever. Respect is the alpha and omega of lasting relationships because it enfolds true love from beginning to end.

Chapter 18
The Final Destination

The Testimony to True Love

Many of us probably know men and women who are living a relationship of true love and who can testify to the reality of true love with their lives — blessing and enriching our own journeys by their display of enduring togetherness. We would like to share the blessing of one such couple.

Sue and John met on a blind date while attending neighboring colleges in New York City. Sue was a freshman and John was a sophomore. Sue's cousin, who was dating John's brother, wanted Sue to come on a double date. John's brother chose John to come along, somewhat by default. The reality of this meeting seemed somewhat mystical, in fact, since Sue had always planned to attend college in Boston along with her friends. But during some point in her decision-making process, she felt drawn to do something "different" than the rest of the crowd and headed to New York.

Their blind date was pure fun and they came away with an awareness of feeling extremely comfortable with each other. They talked, laughed, sang and acted silly together at a restaurant crowded with college students. They felt a subtle "click," not the fireworks of love at first sight, but the satisfaction of being comfortable and having enjoyed the time spent with each other.

It wasn't until a month or two later, when John needed a date for a dance, that he called Sue. This evening together marked a clearer beginning of their relationship, and although no flying rockets and fireworks exploded, they felt attracted to one another. Sue thought, "Hey, I'd like to get to know this guy."

Sue and John got together every week or so. Given the lack of money common to a couple of college kids, their time was usually spent walking and talking about anything and everything. They discovered similarities in their values, feelings and experiences related to school, family, friends and the like, and always felt a freedom to share their thoughts without holding back. One of their favorite things was to spend a day in Central Park just sitting next to one another, writing letters or reading. They felt a connection just sitting in each other's presence.

For the first year and a half of their relationship, Sue and John continued to expand their common interests, realizing they were beginning to like what each other liked and felt a frequent longing to be together. They saw each other every weekend, talked and sent letters during the week. After about a year and a half of dating, Sue began to realize that she desired a deeper mutual commitment with John. She wanted to know him and his feelings more intimately and wanted him to know the same about her. She told John of her desires for closeness, wishing she could "be inside his mind," and he agreed that he wanted to know her in the same way. This was an exciting time for them. They had become best friends and now they were beginning to know each other more deeply as persons. They experienced a dynamic sense of growing together.

John and Sue had both decided early on that their growing emotional intimacy required a decision not to have sexual relations. While perhaps not totally aware of why they did not want to be sexually active, they were clear that they had a very deep respect for one another and did not want to jeopardize that respect by becoming sexually involved. This was often a difficult decision to live out, given their intensifying emotional closeness and the frequent opportunities to be alone. But both of them knew they were not ready for the responsibilities and level of commitment that a sexual relationship would bring. They knew that there was always the possibility that, regardless of how much they loved each other, they could still end up journeying with someone else for the whole of life. Their values also played a role in their decision for chastity. John and Sue had both grown up Catholic, and although they were active in their faith to varying degrees at different times, the value base of their family and faith experiences contributed — in usually unconscious ways — to their choice to wait for sex until marriage.

Living out this decision also challenged them to grow in their relationship as they had a desire to reach a commitment of betrothed love and deepened their friendship through further actions of respect, kindness, fun, working together and support. Sue's typing papers for John or John's riding the bus with Sue to her dorm at 3:00 A.M. to be sure she was safe were reflections of how they focused on what each other needed and deepened their friendship. In many ways, they were living for each other without ever experiencing a sense of being used or taken for granted.

By the time John graduated from college and moved to Connecticut for his first job, he and Sue had become soul mates, truly best friends on the journey of love. They communicated every bit of what was on their minds and in their hearts and were able to do this knowing they would not be judged insensitively or pushed away. They trusted each other completely, solved problems together and sensed that they were beginning to touch each other's souls even more deeply.

The separation that followed John's graduation was hard on both of them, but it helped to strengthen their relationship. They had a "soul awareness" that they would marry someday, even though they had not often spoken about marriage. Several months after Sue graduated from college, she was somewhat surprised when John gave her an engagement ring and asked her to marry him. She knew it was the right thing to do since their soul-sharing connection and presence to each other had matured into betrothed love and desire for a lifelong commitment. They were best friends and best companions already, fitting together in so many ways that marriage and the dreams of family life were a natural next step on their journey. Sue's wise but humorous great-aunt had always told her that "you'll know you love someone if you can use his toothbrush," and with John, the answer was "yes."

While their engagement and wedding were wonderful times, in the early years of their marriage they faced many challenges, including the death of John's mother, financial hardship, Sue's first job as a teacher, John's returning to school for his CPA and a struggle with infertility and the humiliations of infertility treatments. Sue and John's commitment to one another never wavered through these times of potential disillusionment, and they remained steadied by their foundation of communication and friendship, doing whatever they needed to do and facing these challenges together. Just like the early days in Central Park, they remained side by side. Their presence, intimacy and connection to one another was a testimony to the love they shared — a full, complete and unconditional love that enriched and expanded their best friendship and experience as soul mates.

As miracles often happen, just as Sue and John were ready to pursue adopting a child, Sue became pregnant. Their love, which began as a sense of comfort, had now become incarnated in the gift of this new life. Within several years, their family was a fivesome — John, Sue, Jack, Dan,

and Mary Kate. The ebb and flow of family life with kids and John's increasing work demands led to the changing currents common to lifetime loves, from the joy of friendship to the passion of lovers to the picture of teammates working together for the kids. Sue and John's enjoyment of being near to one another and the celebrations of their closeness never disappeared.

The Depths of True Love

Have you ever sat on an ocean beach and considered how vast the sea truly is? The sea is so much more than the roll of a wave and the splash of the surf on the sand. Its depth and breadth, so beyond our view, make it impossible to truly know its expanse without experiencing it in some way. The rhythm of the tide at the seashore gives us a hint of what lies beyond our view. As low tide approaches, that which is hidden beneath the surface at high tide is revealed, allowing us to see rocks and shells, mussels, barnacles, hermit crabs and seaweed. The greater the pull of the moon, the lower the tide; the lower the tide, the more we see. There is an abundance of life under high tide's cover that we can only come to know and appreciate when the waters of the sea retreat.

So it is in love's journey. At times love can be low in our relationships, often the result of stress, disappointment or disillusionment. Just like being at the beach at low tide, do we stay in the relationship and explore what is uncovered, or do we leave and go home?

Sue and John's journey required they face stress and pain when, after several months of illness, John was diagnosed with pancreatic cancer. Throughout the months of tests, more tests, consultations and surgery, with the accompanying feelings of shock, fear, hope and sadness, Sue and John lived their relationship the same way they had always lived it — together. The gifts of communication, closeness and faith they had given to each other since the early weeks of their relationship continued to nurture their journey, as they fought to balance...the hope that healing would come, and, if not, that acceptance would follow. Sadly for Sue and John, for their children and for all who knew them, physical healing did not come, but still Sue and John walked on. Together they decided that John would remain at home so that the family could be present to one another during his dying process, a decision that seemed natural when you think of their love's journey. The long nights, the suffering, the goodbyes, were unspeakably difficult, but their commitment to love unconditionally and to trust in God allowed Sue and John to explore dimensions of love's seashore that many lovers never see.

The months since John's death have brought profound sadness and countless tears for Sue, but she often finds that these moments end in a smile arising from her awareness that John is still present to her. His presence is not the physical one of days past; rather she feels John's presence in the whispers of her heart, in the essence of her being. "We knew each other so well," she says, "his presence is still here. He is here in my heart forever."

No Greater Love

We can look back on Sue and John's relationship and see the ways in which their journey followed God's design for the journey of true love. They would humbly be the first to say their love was not perfect, and, of course, no one's is perfect. If not perfect, however, their love was sacramental — it reflected God's love in the world in the way it has been complete, unconditional and permanent. Jesus said, "Greater love than this no man has — to lay down his life for his friends" (Jn 15:13). Sue and John laid down their lives for each other, just as Jesus laid down his life for us. When we give up our lives, however, we find them.

Perhaps the knowledge of Sue and John's journey of love and others like them who experience such a difficult loss is one of the reasons many of us walk away from the path of true love's journey. As much as we know the journey can bring the greatest of joys, we know that it can also bring the greatest of sorrows. "Why," we ask, "should I take such a risk when the journey can end in that way?"

Such a question would be reasonable except for one misunderstanding: the journey doesn't end.

Destination: God

We've spoken of the journey throughout this book as the journey toward lasting relationships, the journey toward true love. In Sue's experience, she knows that John's spirit lives on in her heart because she knows he is with God, continuing his journey and waiting for her there. The journey toward true love brings us together with another person in a lifetime of love, but that is not our ultimate destination. Our true destination is God.

God is love (1 Jn 4:18); therefore, the journey toward true love is the journey toward God. This journey is one of transformation. Love transforms us here on earth in ways that allow us to fulfill our potential as persons created in the image and likeness of God so that after the days of our earthly journey are over, we can continue the journey of love with God in our eternal spiritual home. Our final experience of true love is the fulfillment of soul-sharing intimacy with God. This is the background of love's big picture. God's love for us is complete, unconditional and forever — not only until we die.

Truth, Faith and the Commandment to Love

The transformation necessary for our journey to God starts with our journey here on earth. We hope that these pages have provided you with some insights about what is needed to facilitate one's human journey of love. If we were to summarize and condense everything we've touched on into one single, all-encompassing trail marker, it would read: If you seek true love, seek God, for God is love. Love is a gift from God, and we have God's promise that if we will only love him and do what he asks of us, he will give us what we need for our lives to be joy-filled: "If you love me, you will keep my commandments, and I will ask the Father and he will give you another Intercessor to be with you forever, the Spirit of truth" (Jn 14:15–17).

The gift of the Holy Spirit will provide us with the equipment we need to live out love relationships successfully and journey toward God. This equipment includes the tools of healthy relationships — the fruits of the Spirit within us: kindness, peace, patience, charity, goodness, gentleness, generosity, faithfulness, modesty, joy, self-control and chastity.[1] These are keys that unlock the doors to the truth of our hearts — the presence of God's love in each of us that allows us to love others in the image of God.

Standing before Pilate, Jesus made it clear that he came to earth to testify to the truth. This truth is the truth of God's love, which will free us from the bondage of sin and death. Will this truth simply come up and knock on our door one day? No, it won't. Jesus said that those of us who are committed to the truth will hear his voice (Jn 18:37–38). Hearing his voice, his truth, is not easy for many of us, so Jesus described the listening process: "If you abide in my word, you're truly disciples of mine, and you'll know the truth, and the truth will set you free" (Jn 8:31–32).

To be free — that is, free to choose God as our beloved — comes from knowing the truth. Knowing the truth is a result of living the way Jesus asks us to live and loving the way he asks us to love. Jesus' instructions on how to love are extremely concise:

"This is my commandment: love one another as I have loved you" (Jn 15:12).

We are called to testify to the truth of love by loving as God loves: completely, unconditionally and permanently.

God created us to love faithfully, and we are called to love with our hearts and feelings, with our minds and choices, with our bodies and actions, with our spirits and faith. In other words, we are called to love with our entire being. Why? Because in the end, God wants us back with him.

"So these three — faith, hope, and love — remain, but the greatest of them all is love" (1 Cor 13:13).

Notes

Orientation

1. William Maestri, *What the Church Teaches, A Guide for the Study of Educational Guidance in Human Love* (Boston: Pauline Books & Media, 1996), 61.

2. Pope John Paul II, *Love and Responsibility* (New York: Farrar, Straus and Giroux, 1981), 83.

3. Maestri, *What the Church Teaches.*

Preparations for the Journey

1. G. Chapman, *The Five Love Languages: How to Express Heartfelt Commitment to Your Mate* (Chicago: Northfield, 1992).

2. J. Beck, *Cognitive Therapy: Basics and Beyond* (New York: Guilford, 1995).

3. J. Young, *Cognitive Therapy for Personality Disorders: A Schema Focused Approach* (Sarasota: Professional Resource Exchange, 1990).

4. Beck, *Cognitive Therapy.*

5. Pope John Paul II, *Love and Responsibility,* 48.

6. William Bausch, *Becoming a Man* (Mystic, CT: Twenty-Third Publications, 1988), 81.

7. Pope John Paul II, *Love and Responsibility,* 46.

8. Ibid., 47.

9. Ibid., 50.

10. Ibid., 60–61.

11. Ibid., 75–76.

12. Ibid., 78.

13. Ibid., 77–79.

14. Ibid., 79.

15. Ibid., 80–81.

16. Ibid., 82–83.

17. Ibid., 84.

18. Ibid., 85–87.

19. Ibid., 92.

20. Ibid., 90–93.

21. Ibid., 95–97.

22. Ibid., 97.

23. Ibid., 100.

Experiencing the Journey

1. Bausch, *Becoming a Man,* 198.

2. John Kippley, *Sex and the Marriage Covenant* (Cincinnati: Couple to Couple League, 1991), 27.

3. Peter the Hermit, as quoted by C. Cullen, in T. McGrath, *At Home With Our Faith* (Chicago: Claretian Publications, 1999), 2.

4. U.S. Catholic Bishops, *Human Sexuality: A Catholic Perspective on Lifelong Learning* (Washington, DC: United States Catholic Conference, 1990), 19.

5. The Holy See, *Catechism of the Catholic Church* (Boston: Pauline Books & Media, 1994), nn. 2337–2345.

6. The Pontifical Council for the Family, *The Truth and Meaning of Human Sexuality: Guidelines for Education within the Family* (Boston: Pauline Books & Media, 1995), n. 4.

7. Pope John Paul II, *Apostolic Exhortation on the Role of the Christian Family in the Modern World (Familiaris Consortio)* (Boston: Pauline Books & Media, 1982), 54–55.

8. C. E. Koop, as quoted in the brochure "Is There Real Safe Sex?" (Spokane, WA: Teen Aid).

9. *Facts in Brief* (New York: The Alan Guttmacher Institute, 1993). See also National Institutes of Health, *Fact Sheet* (Bethesda, MD: U.S. Department of Health and Human Services, 1998), available on the Internet at: http://www.niaid.nih.gov/factsheets/stdstats.htm

10. E. Jones and J. Forrest, "Contraceptive Failure in the U.S.," *Family Planning Perspectives* 21, no. 3 (1989); S. Weller, "A Meta-analysis of Condom Effectiveness in Reducing Sexually Transmitted HIV," *Social Science and Medicine* 36, no. 12 (1993); K. Noller, *OB/GYN Clinical Alert* (September, 1992).

11. J. McIlleney, "The Facts About the Sexually Transmitted Disease Epidemic." Brochure published by the Medical Institute for Sexual Health,

Austin, Texas; Institute of Medicine, *The Hidden Epidemic: Confronting Sexually Transmitted Diseases* (Washington, DC: National Academy, 1997).

12. R. Levin, "The Redbook Report on Premarital and Extramarital Sex: The End of the Double Standard?" *Redbook* (October 1975): 40; A. Demaris and K. Rao, "Premarital Cohabitation and Subsequent Marital Stability in the U.S.: A Reassessment," *Journal of Marriage and the Family* 54 (1992): 178.

13. W. Mattox Jr., "What's Marriage Got to Do With It?" *Family Policy* 6, no. 6 (February 1994); Family Research Council, "National Family Values: A Survey of Adults," May 1994.

14. CT Information Research Department, "Christianity Today: Marriage and Divorce Survey Report," July 1992.

15. D. Whitman, "Was It Good for Us?" *U.S. News and World Report* (May 19, 1997): 59.

16. N. Bennet, A. Blanc and D. Bloom, "Commitment and the Modern Union: Assessing the Link Between Premarital Cohabitation and Subsequent Marital Stability," *American Sociological Review* 53 (1988): 127–138.

17. P. Blumstein and P. Schwartz, *American Couples: Money, Work and Sex* (New York: William Morrow, 1983).

18. K. Furste and K. Tanfer, "Sexual Exclusivity among Dating, Cohabitating and Married Women," *Journal of Marriage and the Family* 58 (1996): 33–47.

19. Blumstein and Schwartz, *American Couples*.

20. Whitman, "Was It Good for Us?" 60; L. Bumpass, J. Sweet and A. Cherlin, "The Role of Cohabitation in Declining Rates of Marriage," *Journal of Marriage and the Family* 53 (1991): 913–927.

21. E. Thomson and V. Colella, "Cohabitation and Marital Stability: Quality or Commitment?" *Journal of Marriage and the Family* 54 (1992): 259–267; Demaris and Rao, "Premarital Cohabitation."

22. J. Teachman and K. Paasik, "Legal Status and the Stability of Coresidential Unions," *Demography* 28 (1991): 571.

23. D. Whitman, "Was It Good for Us?" 60.

24. For the pope's teaching on the theology of the body, see Pope John Paul II, *The Theology of the Body: Human Love in the Divine Plan* (Boston: Pauline Books & Media, 1997); see also Kippley, *Sex and the Marriage Covenant*.

25. Pope John Paul II, *Familiaris Consortio*, 25.

26. U.S. Bishops, *Human Sexuality*, 55.

27. Y. Schneider, "The Gay Gene: Going, Going...Gone," *Insight* no. 218, Family Research Council, 2000.

28. T. Dailey and C. Roberts,"The Facts About 'Just the Facts.'" *Insight* no. 207, Family Research Council, 1999; Julia Duin, "New Psychiatric Study Says Gays Can Alter Orientation," *The Washington Times*, May 9, 2001.

29. *Catechism of the Catholic Church*, no. 2351.

30. Kippley, *Sex and the Marriage Covenant*, 14.

31. Tom Ehart, *Dating, Sex, Me and God* (Boston: Pauline Books & Media, 1995), 52.

32. J. Newman, "Proud to Be a Virgin," *New York Times*, June 19, 1994, sec. 9; "Changes in Sexual Permissiveness," *GSS News*, no. 6 (September 1992): 4–6.

33. Whitman, "Was It Good for Us?" 58; D. Michael, "Sexuality: When Is It Too Much of a Good Thing?" *Register Report* 25 (1999): 3.

34. M. Clements, *Parade*, August 7, 1994, 4–5.

35. P. Driscoll, *Sex Appreciation: A Handbook on Chastity* (Pleasant Hill, CA: Womanity, 1988), 50.

36. S. Walen, R. DiGuiseppe and R. Wessler, *A Practioner's Guide to Rational Emotive Therapy* (New York: Oxford University Press, 1980), 116–125.

37. *Diagnostic and Statistical Manual of Mental Disorders* (Washington, DC: American Psychiatric Association, 1994), 327.

38. A. Beck, A. Rush, B. Shaw and G. Emery, *Cognitive Therapy of Depression* (New York: Guilford, 1979), 11.

39. R. Flannery, *Post-Traumatic Stress Disorder: The Victim's Guide to Healing and Recovery* (New York: Crossroad, 1993), 87–108.

40. Copper Country Sexual Assault Survivor Services, "Here Are Useful Facts About Rape and Sexual Assault." [online database], www.mint.net/rrs/Information.htm.

41. Ibid.

42. Earth Operations Central, "Rohypnol Alert Page." [online database], http://earthops.org/rohypnol.html.

The Journey Home

1. *Catechism of the Catholic Church*, no. 1832.

Further Reading for the Journey

Relationship With God

N. J. Wright. *The Challenge of Jesus: Rediscovering Who Jesus Was and Is.* InterVarsity.

C. Colson and N. Pearcey. *How Now Shall We Live?* Tyndale House.

H. Blackaby and C. King. *Experiencing God: Knowing and Doing His Will.* Broadman and Holman.

Papal Documents

Pope John Paul II. *The Role of the Christian Family in the Modern World (Familiaris Consortio).* Pauline Books & Media.

Pope John Paul II. *The Theology of the Body: Human Love in the Divine Plan.* Pauline Books & Media.

Pope Paul VI. *Of Human Life (Humanae Vitae).* Pauline Books & Media.

Books on Relationship and Sexuality

L. Parrott and L. Parrott. *Saving Your Marriage Before It Starts.* Zondervan.

J. Harris and R. St. James. *I Kissed Dating Goodbye.*
Multnomah.

H. Cloud and Dr. J. Townsend. *Boundaries in Dating.*
Zondervan.

J. Kippley. *Sex and the Marriage Covenant.* Couple to Couple
League.

T. Ehart. *Dating, Sex, Me and God.* Pauline Books & Media.

M. Blaine Smith. *Should I Get Married?* InterVarsity.

T. Finn and D. Finn. *Intimate Bedfellows: Love, Sex and the
Catholic Church.* Pauline Books & Media.

Emotions and Self-Esteem

D. Burns. *The Feeling Good Handbook.* Plume.

J. Beck. *Behavior Therapy and Beyond.* Guilford.

Homosexuality

J. Nicolosi. *Reparative Therapy and the Male Homosexual.* Jason
Aronson.

E. Moberly. *Homosexuality. A New Christian Ethic.* Lut-
terworth.

J. Harvey. *The Truth About Homosexuality.* Ignatius Press.

Support Programs

Courage, a support ministry for Catholic homosexuals, can
usually be contacted through your parish or diocese.
Their national office is located at: St. John the Baptist
Church, 210 West 31st Street, New York, NY 10001; 212–
268–1010; http://CourageRC.org

Exodus International. A nondenominational support
ministry based in San Rafael, CA; http://www.exodus-
intl.org

Personal Notes:

Pauline
BOOKS & MEDIA

The Daughters of St. Paul operate book and media centers at the following addresses. Visit, call or write the one nearest you today, or find us on the World Wide Web, www.pauline.org

CALIFORNIA
3908 Sepulveda Blvd, Culver City, CA 90230   310-397-8676
5945 Balboa Avenue, San Diego, CA 92111   858-565-9181
46 Geary Street, San Francisco, CA 94108   415-781-5180

FLORIDA
145 S.W. 107th Avenue, Miami, FL 33174   305-559-6715

HAWAII
1143 Bishop Street, Honolulu, HI 96813   808-521-2731
Neighbor Islands call: 800-259-8463

ILLINOIS
172 North Michigan Avenue, Chicago, IL 60601   312-346-4228

LOUISIANA
4403 Veterans Memorial Blvd, Metairie, LA 70006   504-887-7631

MASSACHUSETTS
Rte. 1, 885 Providence Hwy, Dedham, MA 02026   781-326-5385

MISSOURI
9804 Watson Road, St. Louis, MO 63126   314-965-3512

NEW JERSEY
561 U.S. Route 1, Wick Plaza, Edison, NJ 08817   732-572-1200

NEW YORK
150 East 52nd Street, New York, NY 10022   212-754-1110
78 Fort Place, Staten Island, NY 10301   718-447-5071

OHIO
2105 Ontario Street, Cleveland, OH 44115   216-621-9427

PENNSYLVANIA
9171-A Roosevelt Blvd, Philadelphia, PA 19114   215-676-9494

SOUTH CAROLINA
243 King Street, Charleston, SC 29401   843-577-0175

TENNESSEE
4811 Poplar Avenue, Memphis, TN 38117   901-761-2987

TEXAS
114 Main Plaza, San Antonio, TX 78205   210-224-8101

VIRGINIA
1025 King Street, Alexandria, VA 22314   703-549-3806

CANADA
3022 Dufferin Street, Toronto, Ontario, Canada M6B 3T5   416-781-9131
1155 Yonge Street, Toronto, Ontario, Canada M4T 1W2   416-934-3440

¡También somos su fuente para libros, videos y música en español!